# THE DIGITAL CREATIVE'S SURVIVAL GUIDE

# THE DIGITAL CREATIVE'S SURVIVAL GUIDE

Paul Wyatt

Cincinnati, Ohio
www.howdesign.com

 Published by HOW Books, an imprint of F+W Media, Inc., 10151 Carver Road, Suite 200, Blue Ash, Ohio 45242. (800) 289-0963. First edition.

For more excellent books and resources for designers, visit www.howdesign.com.

17 16 15 14 13 5 4 3 2 1

ISBN-13: 978-1-4403-1848-1

Distributed in Canada by Fraser Direct
100 Armstrong Avenue
Georgetown, Ontario, Canada L7G 5S4
Tel: (905) 877-4411

Distributed in the U.K. and Europe by F&W Media International, LTD
Brunel House, Forde Close, Newton Abbot, TQ12 4PU, UK
Tel: (+44) 1626 323200, Fax: (+44) 1626 323319
Email: enquiries@fwmedia.com

Distributed in Australia by Capricorn Link
P.O. Box 704, Windsor, NSW 2756 Australia
Tel: (02) 4560-1600

Edited by Scott Francis
Designed by Ronson Slagle
Production coordinated by Greg Nock

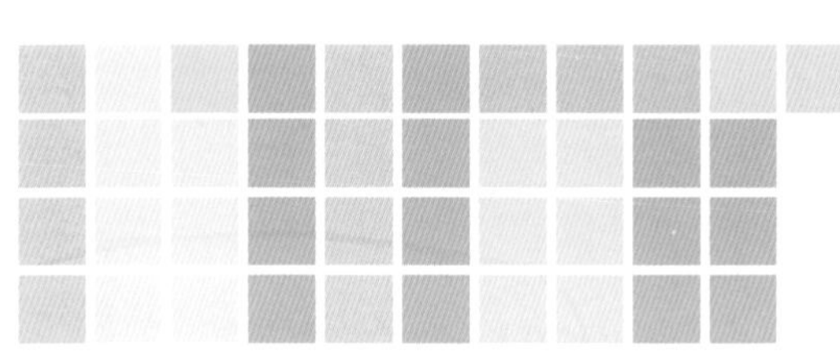

# Acknowledgments

*Love and thanks to Delia and Joseph Wyatt for being creative parents and for putting up with a boy who wanted to fly to the moon. To my sister Julie for her Madonna-favored creative brilliances and to Luke Prowse for joyful happy grumpy times.*

*Thanks to all the creatives who either publicly or anonymously contributed material to this book. Thanks to Helen Jones for all her wonderful help with material supplied from The Partners, Maya Hart at Landor London, Kate Towey at magneticNorth, Janet Moses at Why Not Associates, Steve Bittan at Ustwo and Rod Plummer and Victoria Hammond at Shoothill.*

*Matt Holding did a fine job as researcher on this title, sifting through facts and interviews and having to put up with my old-fashioned dial phone. Thanks to him and Joseph Luck, who with me form Three Men and a Camera, the work of which is featured in this book.*

# Contents

# dig·i·tal cre·a·tive

*noun*

**1.** A person engaged in a profession or activity that is performed using digital devices; especially: a digital designer, web designer, motion graphics specialist, animator, videographer, typographer, packaging designer, illustrator, developer, etc.

**2.** The output of the person described in the definition above

# Introduction

**WORKING IN THE CREATIVE INDUSTRY** is a fantastically rewarding experience. Making digital handicrafts, such as a website, a piece of digital design, a film, an animation or anything else that goes under the "creative" banner, is the ultimate in creative expression. As creative practitioners, there's a thrill we all experience from making something out of nothing.

Sadly, there's no manual for a career in creative. From the outside in, you'd imagine it's a world of beer fridges, beards, creative posturing and pop-up ideas, which is usually the impression given when fellow creatives discuss their work.

This self-mythologizing perpetuates the idea that we all spend most of our time playing foosball and drawing pretty pictures. We don't normally communicate the long hours and the sheer difficulty at times of giving birth to an idea. What is forgotten is that the creative industry is a commercial enterprise. Part of our job is to help people sell stuff like washing machines, apps and concert tickets. We have client briefs to follow and interpret and add our own creative spin to.

Dealing with politics, clients and that annoying guy you sit next to who bounces a ball off a wall when he's thinking is something that's never taught at college. Neither is dealing with project management or asking for a needed pay raise. Just because we happen to be in a creative career where we make things out of pixels doesn't mean we do it for fun alone.

The idea behind this book was to put together a manual to help creatives get through the nitty-gritty of creative life and understand the business around them. In this book, I try to offer perspective and guidance to help you:

- understand that clients aren't mad
- post rational ideas
- deal with ego (your own and your boss's)
- deal with harsh criticism

I've done my best to come up with some straightforward, fluff-free insight and advice for working in the digital creative field.

I didn't just want it to be my voice in these pages, so I wrote to some great creatives in this profession—people I'd worked with as a designer and as a creative director—seeking pearls of wisdom, anecdotes and advice for dealing with the joys, highs and lows of creative life. An avalanche of replies came through with nuggets of information and details of how best to forge a path to a successful and creatively inspiring working life. This business throws up challenges left, right and center. Everyone in the world has a degree of creativity in their DNA, and because of that they're all your critics. Learning to deal with creative people is as important as being creative in your job. This book will give you some valued insider knowledge, inspiration and a few sneaky tricks to help you through your life as a digital creative.

# Being Creative

# Horses for courses: Finding the right creative outlet for you

**UNFORTUNATELY**, money makes the world go round, and unless you're privileged enough to have a trust fund, a large inheritance or some friendly soul who sugars your life with cash, you'll need to find a commercial outlet for your talents.

If the thought of going solo with freelancing or setting up your own business fills you with horror then there are two other routes you can choose: working for a creative agency where you work across multiple brands, or working client-side (or "in house" as it's also called) where you work for one brand only.

Both of these types of work have misconceptions surrounding them. Working agency-side is often considered creatively better. Or in real terms it's considered "cooler." You'll go to work in a fabulous creative space, work with household brands, have a say at every creative turn and wear clear glass spectacles and ironic-slogan T-shirts. Fridays are "why days," and you'll spend most of the afternoon in the beer fridge. It sounds heavenly.

Working client-side, on the other hand, is for those who just don't cut it creatively. These poor individuals scrape a living together using their limited talent to churn out banners, websites and, if they're lucky, the company Christmas card. They work for marketing managers who are either failed or frustrated designers, and no one really cares if you do a good job or not as long as you throw something together by the end of the day.

These are the popular misconceptions, but they do hold some nuggets of truth and are usually spouted by agency designers who've never worked client-side and client-side people who've never been anywhere near an agency. Talentwise, you'll find the great and good on both sides, but the snobbery that exists between the two usually unravels itself when you have a closer look at the benefits of both types of working.

> “It was a great lesson to never forget the end user, as we’re not doing this for self-indulgence; we’re doing it for a commercial value. So it taught me to think about what the motivations of the customer are.

## Thriving client-side

Peter Knapp, executive creative director at Landor London—one of the biggest creative powerhouses in the world—started his career client-side at Dixons, the UK electrical retailer, in their in-house design studio. There he learned about the hard school of retail and the high street. “It was a great lesson to never forget the end user, as we’re not doing this for self-indulgence; we’re doing it for a commercial value. So it taught me to think about what the motivations of the customer are.”

Understanding the end user and their needs and wants in any brief is an essential and transferable skill. Working client-side is a great grounding for learning the practicalities of business, as you’re right there in the firing line. If something isn’t working with the business—if sales are low and if the ads on the website aren’t performing—you’ll be one of the first to hear about it. In an agency, you’re a little more buffered from this. It’s a case of Chinese whispers how feedback comes down the line. At client-side you get to see how all the cogs of the business work and the immediate impact your work has on them. This helps keep in mind how and why people are interacting with your product or service, and you’ll learn an awful lot about the mechanics of a brand and the business as a whole. These skills are essential and transferable to your career, for making the leap to running your own creative setup or moving across to an agency.

“I’d say it can be a good start doing client-side stuff for a bit,” says Paul Davis of Overthrow Productions Limited. “But I wouldn’t stick around in an environment where creatively you’re just churning out the same old stuff year after year for too long.”

That’s sound advice, but if you’re

— Peter Knapp, executive creative director, Landor London

creatively restless and have taken a client-side job because no agency was hiring and you want to jump across in the future, then you should make the most of the opportunity at hand. Creatively restless people don't ever just "churn out" work. If they do so then it's their own fault. Author Ruth Burke once said, "Only boring people get bored," and it works the same way with creatives who say the work they're given is creatively uninspiring. Designers who find themselves in a creative rut need to look for challenges within that constraint. If you can demonstrate that ability, you'll do well agency-side, client-side or even when setting up your own business as a freelancer or in a collective.

Usually at client-side, you'll have a flatter structure and whatever your level in the company you should be able to look for ways of making the work more exciting. You're the guardian of the brand guidelines, so break them where you can. The client-side designer probably has much more creative freedom than their agency counterpart. It's all a matter of how you apply and push yourself. Look at using downtime to work on self-initiated projects that will creatively enhance the brand (and your time spent there), and present these to your marketing or creative manager. Don't be a drone. If you are, you're probably in the wrong business. Make a difference to the brand and stamp your mark. It will prove to be invaluable experience further along your career.

I spent part of the dot com boom working client-side at a large Internet portal. Everything was going digital, and at the time it was easier to find a client-side "digital department" (or "e-division" as they were sometimes questionably called) than a digital creative agency. There were very few of these in Britain at the time.

**“ There seems to be opinion floating around that working client-side is the kiss of death for a designer. Don’t assume ‘client-side’ means working for a big brand; there are hundreds of start-ups out there doing interesting things in need of good designers.**

It did aesthetically feel like working in accountancy, and every few weeks I’d be summoned to the managing director’s office to justify the existence of the creative team. But the collaborative work and experience I gained there has shaped my career significantly.

Rather than having worked with “failed” creatives, as the client-side myth would have you believe, I worked with some of the best. Luke Prowse is now well known for having been legendary art director Neville Brody’s “right-hand man” on projects such as the redesign of *The Times*, as well as working in graphic and web creative for many luxury brands. I was also working with Tom Baker who has become an animation director and has worked on the BAFTA Award-nominated *Skatoony* for Cartoon Network and mini animated epics such as *Heavenly Sword* (which was released as a tie in to the Heavenly Sword video game). None of us wanted to be stuck making animated banners or updating web pages. It was duller than ditchwater, but we knew the way around it was to use downtime to develop new skills. I had an interest in motion and video, Tom in animation and Luke in typography and code design.

We pooled this skill set together, and whenever a design request would come in, we’d turn it on its head and present back a much more creatively challenging brief. You have to remember that in some client-side offices, the people briefing you spend most of the day absorbed in spreadsheets. They’re a bit fearful of the “designer” and usually say such things as, “Don’t be too creative” or “I don’t care what it sounds or looks like as

— Tom Harding, interaction designer, Made by Many

long as it gets done." It's a little like asking a chef to boil an egg. All day. Every day. Breaking that cycle takes confidence in your abilities and a desire to produce interesting work. It also takes assurances to the person briefing you that it won't take any more time, cost any more money or make them look silly. If you're making those promises, then make sure you make them stick—else you'll never be able to convince them again. We would always say we could do something, they'd agree, and we'd then rush off and learn how to get it done.

The company we were working for was owned by one of the world's largest publishers of music and DVDs. It also had its fingers in the broadcast world. We'd become known as the team that was cheap, good and useful, and we were soon in demand—producing animations for DVDs, campaigns for global album releases, websites for TV shows, product videos and short films. I strongly believe that if you say you can do something, then you're one step on the path to actually getting it done.

"There seems to be opinion floating around that working client-side is the kiss of death for a designer. Don't assume 'client-side' means working for a big brand; there are hundreds of start-ups out there doing interesting things in need of good designers," advises Tom Harding, interaction designer at the innovative products and services agency Made by Many. "When I worked for a start-up, I gained a lot of experience that set me up for the future. Often being client-side you are closer to your users and gain insights into how people interact with your designs. I learned a lot about agile and lean development and

> **Agency life offers a fantastic mix of work, along with the chance to enjoy a vibrant social culture. I'd say that our industry, as much as most, places great importance on working hard but playing hard, too.**

gained important understandings of how a business works. All these are transferable skills that agencies should be looking for in a good designer."

Oh, and if you're still of the opinion that working client-side can be creatively stifling, Ben Curzon reminds me that Jonathan Ive, the designer of the iMac, iPhone, PowerBook G4 and a host of other Apple products, is indeed a client-side designer.

Office politics client-side can be slightly rougher than those found in an agency. During research for this book, a few industrious and highly creative client-side workers told me they'd found themselves rather shockingly made redundant. This mostly came down to transparency. In a client-side set up, it's important to communicate the value creative adds to the business. If that's not communicated, the creative team will always be on the chopping block for resources. In an agency, everyone knows the value of creative, as it's the lifeblood of the business that pays everybody's wages.

The way to deal with the client-side issue of transparency is to produce a quarterly, visuals-only presentation of work. This should be presented in a companywide meeting, making it clear what was produced and for which department. This creates transparency about the work produced and its overall value. If possible, have each member of the team present their own work, which will raise their profile and ensure everyone knows what they do for the company.

Cram this presentation with visuals to make clear the value this creative team has lended to all the departments that have used it as a resource. This pretty much makes the team bulletproof. This also works in larger agencies where you have different

— Leon Bahrani, senior designer, The Partners

divisions such as "Digital," "Print" and "Motion," which are led by different creative directors. A transparency presentation puts everyone on the same page and stops wagging tongues asking, "What exactly do they do?"

## Agency side

Agencies vary wildly in size, culture and in their approach to solving creative problems. "If you believe and share their ethos, agencies are great," says Ross Fordham, design director at The Partners. "They can act as an amazing platform to grow from, with a wealth of experience you can continually mine."

Smaller agencies are great if you want to hit the ground running as a junior and be involved in lots of different projects. They are most certainly a breath of fresh air if you have been working for a while in a larger agency with rigid hierarchies and processes.

Smaller agencies have an organized sense and feel of college life camaraderie to them. You'll find that the founders of these have usually paid their dues working at the larger creative factories and have created working environments that are more playful, supportive, relaxed and conducive to creative work.

The temptation is to dive into a big top ten rated agency and stay there because they're the ones producing all the great work. Not so. A smaller agency is more of an attractive proposition to a client, as they'll get to meet everyone on the account: the account managers, the designers, the coders and everyone in between. There's more of a direct relationship with the client, as they feel more comfortable and have an easier flow of communication. This flatter structure and shared joy of working collaboratively reaps benefits in the end product. Quite frankly, ideas can come from anywhere, and if you're in an environment that is receptive and responsive, it doesn't matter if the idea starts with Alice the cleaner as long as it starts somewhere. As the creative director, it's important to recognize people who work well together and not to feel pushed out or intimidated by this. Just let them get on with it. If they're creating great ideas and working well together, this can only benefit the shared joy of having produced a great product for the whole of the team.

The big agencies work in project teams made up of people you might only work with once every few months. This makes it a little awkward in developing a creative flow with people, as you're always starting from scratch. The camaraderie with your fellow workers isn't always there, and it's more a case of "eyes down and churn out the work" in a very pipeline fashion. You may never see a client or have any real input on the work being produced. You just become a cog in a very big wheel. "Some people need to work in larger agencies; they need the comfort of a hierarchical system, and the rewards and job titles, and ego boost of being 'above' other co-workers," says Planning Unit's Jeff Knowles. Certainly juniors at larger creative agencies will spend more time cutting foam board and spray-mounting presentations, unlike their smaller agency or client-side counterparts who have more input into the projects.

At most agencies, you'll be expected to work beyond the normal working hours of nine to five. "A classic line to hear on a Friday that not only ruins your weekend but makes you feel dread for the upcoming week is, 'Hope you haven't planned anything for next week...,'" remarks a designer who preferred to remain anonymous. If you're in an environment and culture that celebrates the end of a long project in which people have put in the hours by taking the team to the pub or pausing to review and thank hard work, it goes a long way to making you feel appreciated and ready to meet other similar challenges. It's great for team building. If you're in an agency with a culture of "joyless excellence," where the staff aren't applauded and it's just straight on to the next brief, then resentment can set in. You'll feel undervalued, which can affect your work, and it's probably time to cut and run and get out of there. An agency that can socialize together will work hard together, as Leon Bahrani, one of the senior designers at The Partners illustrates: "Agency life offers a fantastic mix of work, along with the chance to enjoy a vibrant social culture. I'd say that our industry, as much as most, places great importance on working hard but playing hard, too."

Smaller agencies don't suffer as much from factions or cliques, and this makes them healthier places to work.

So choose an agency with care. Research the work they do and their culture. Also try and find out about staff turnover. If it's high, then think about why that is. A high turnover of staff indicates an unhappy agency culture. If you're a hardened soul and feel hale and hearty enough to deal with the competitive thrust of larger agency life, then the larger, more regimented agency is for you. If you like the idea of being on a smaller team that works hard and produces great creative and bonds well together, then a smaller agency would likely be a better fit. At agency-side, you'll probably have more time for explorative work than at client-side, where it's mostly about delivery and getting it right the first time.

Both client- and agency-side are routes through which you can make a career in creative. They each offer unique challenges and lessons. Of course, within both there are positives and negatives, but that's part and parcel of life. If you're able to make the most of an opportunity and remind yourself of the transferable skills you're gaining whilst doing that, then you'll always be equipped to make the most of any given situation. Whichever route you choose, the important thing to remember is that if you find yourself becoming stale or in a creative rut, then it's time to look at ways of creatively challenging yourself—be it by self-initiated work or stepping out of your comfort zone and trying something new.

# A space to think: How your environment affects your creativity

## Preconceived thoughts

What type of space is the perfect one to be creative in? Is it a quirky loft laden with retro analogue charm? Maybe something with more of an minimalist aesthetic, with white walls, clean surfaces and lots of toys from the Apple store? Perhaps even it's a converted warehouse with stuffed rats, naked shop mannequins and mobility scooters? Don't scoff—all these places exist. They're all creative studios, and although each one is very different, they fall into what we imagine creative spaces to be like, namely anything but a Dilbert-style work cubicle. Let's face it, cubicles are isolation tanks stereotypically thought of as the domain of accountants, administrators and those who have real jobs doing important things for real people.

If you walked into an accountant's office and it was full of lava lamps, foosball tables and people sitting on bean bags, a great big alarm would go off in your head telling you these weren't the people to trust with your income tax return. Sadly, perception is everything. They could in fact be the best accountants in the world, but they've failed to give the right perception of this with a seriously misjudged sense of how to inspire trust and professionalism via their office décor.

Creative studios suffer from a similar preconception. Clients expect their hired designers to sit in working environments

*Workspace of freelance designer Franz Jeitz*

that are certainly more off-the-wall than their own. Any creative agency opting for gray walls and a siloed sense of working will give the impression that if they can't be bothered to use their creativity on their own work space, what are the chances that they'll use it on the client's campaign?

Remember this is only a perception. You could be based in a tiny studio with very little natural light and a view of a brick wall outside your window but produce the most stunning creative work. As a creative, you have lots of preconceived thoughts thrown at you about who you are and what you do, such as being slightly aloof, possibly eccentric, precious and a proponent of skinny jeans. You could spend a very long time trying to change preconceptions, or you could learn to understand and work around them a little.

## Real working spaces

Have you ever been to one of those bars that advertises itself as an "authentic Irish pub"? These "pubs" can be found in downtown areas everywhere, but in Ireland these are kitted out with shamrocks, shillelaghs and armies of leprechauns. They're about as real and authentic as blue mist, with the Irish ephemera coming from a factory in Birmingham. But for the customers who imbibe in them, the establishments have all the accoutrements of an "Irish" experience and play up to their

## *SURVIVING A BAD OFFICE WORK SPACE*
### *(SITTING UP AGAINST A WALL)*

- If you're suffering from hamster-wheel agency creative-space fatigue, try to maintain a sense of calm within the space you can control.
- Think of the creative idea. Try to walk around. Stop staring at that wall and don't panic. Think about your recent inspirations, the film you saw, that thing your girlfriend said, what you liked about the art deco exhibition you saw. Get outside if you can (admittedly awkward at some hamster-wheel agencies, as you can't put "thinking" on your timesheet).
- Remember that people are like mirrors. What you project out about yourself to someone will be reflected back at you a hundred times over. In a large hamster-wheel agency where competition is fierce and finding your voice can be difficult and intimidating, always try to project a positive "Can do; I'm on it"-type persona, even if you've been sitting for months jammed up against a printer in a cramped work space. This attitude will then be reflected back at you and give you confidence to do the work or task set. If you're constantly projecting nervousness or "I'm not sure if I can" or "What if I can't do it right?" out to people who have neither the time nor the inclination to boost your confidence about a job at hand, then they will reflect this back to you and it will ruin your confidence even more. If you tell someone they're an idiot long enough, they end up believing and acting as if they are one. People's perception of you is mostly created by what you give out.
- Sometimes it's hard to stand out from the crowd and make a difference and show your creative clout, so personalize your work space to show what a creative talent you are and how you're not just another worker bee. Buy a large moleskin pad and some decent pens and pencils (wax crayons, drawing dip pens, etc.) and keep them on your desk with your pad open. Take this pad with you everywhere and fill it up with doodles, ideas, sketches, drawings of your cat, dog, great aunt. It doesn't matter what, just be industrious with your creativity. Take the pad into meetings with your creative director and be sure to flick though it to past ideas that might be useful in meeting a brief that has come into the agency. Leave the pad open on your desk when you go to lunch or visit the loo; you'll find people will flick though it when you're not there. This is where you can use a perception trick that you're an industrious creative with a bookload of ideas to actually reinforce the truth that you're an industrious creative with a bookload of ideas.

- No matter if you sit facing a wall, an air duct or the head of IT with your back facing everyone, remember that a creative space should work for you, even if it's just in how you've personalized your desk space or positioned your monitor. It has to feel comfortable and tailored towards your own way of working.
- The "command" positions in any office space are the ones furthest from the door. People who sit here can watch who comes and who goes. The worst position is to be facing a wall and near the door, as sitting here is fraught with potential perception problems. While I was a creative director for a well-known Internet portal, one of the guys on my team had a monitor that was unfortunately on view to the rest of the office. This didn't really matter as he got on with his work, but he would spend his lunchtime eating at his desk and surfing the web. At this time, our managing director would then walk past on a daily basis. His perception that was that this guy was always surfing the web because that's all he ever saw him doing. During management meetings he'd indulge in "idle moaning" and would frequently refer to my teammate as the "guy who surfs the web all day." Idle moaning is dangerous and happens when people are bored and sit around trying to think up things to say in meetings. It can have disastrous effects, and in this case, the management team was under the belief that my teammate was a work-shy layabout. We fixed this problem within the team by taping a DVD disc to the corner of his monitor so that he could see the approaching managing director. He'd then flip to his email or sometimes the MD's biography on the company website—just to really confuse him. Fortunately this was during the dot com boom, and within four weeks we had another managing director.
- If you've just started your career and find yourself in a creative factory where ideas are shelf stacked and the glory of the successful campaign isn't a shared one, you need to remember that it's not like this everywhere. Fortunately, a lot of people who went on to start their own agencies over the last fifteen years have experienced similar setups as the one you're currently in and have created working environments and studio cultures that are far more conducive to collaborative and more joyous working. Pay your dues there, learn some skills and then move on.

> “We just try to keep it comfortable and productive. There’s some nice artwork we’ve collected on the walls and bookshelves of inspiration to dip into whenever you feel the need.

preconceived idea of what an authentic Irish pub should look like.

Similarly, a prefabricated creative studio that has been dressed to impress can come across as overdesigned, quite forced and lacking a bit of heart. Playing to the audience (in this case purely the clients who pass through the front-of-house areas) lacks a certain truth when it doesn’t accurately reflect the vibe, culture and people who do all the work there. Like the very notion of real style: It needs to be effortless to be true.

I learned this the hard way while sitting on a tree stump in the reception of one of London’s top ten creative agencies. The reception area featured a babbling brook, exposed brickwork, lots and lots and lots of top-notch industry awards and a reception desk fashioned from a tree trunk. As I sat amongst the other wood-dwelling creatures (clients, couriers and other interviewees), I wondered if I could be as cool, creative and just downright weird as this agency obviously was. Was I worthy of coming here every day?

Well, yes and no.

Yes, I got the job, but no, I never went into the front-of-house undergrowth again. Entry for the workers was via a side door, up a flight of stairs, turn right, swipe your entry card and you’re in.

This interesting Victorian building, though full of character, was a stark and messy place once inside: rows and rows

– Paul Davis, Overthrow Productions

of what looked like wallpaper tables with higgledy piggledy seats placed around them and Macs plonked on top. Alongside the walls were giant foam boards with work in progress pinned to them. This was a company that was tentatively embracing digital and held the belief that printing out everything they did to show staff and clients made digital more "real." Cue endless painful discussions with clients who would complain their red logo was coming out a little orange because an RGB logo had been run out of an inkjet printer. There was so much printed out on a daily basis and with no recycling whatsoever, it was only a question of time before the reception's woodland was threatened with the chop to make even more paper. There was very little hustle and bustle. No music, no chat about last night's TV, few smiles and an overbearing atmosphere of joyless excellence. Not the best place to spend 60-plus hours a week. They were slavishly creative and very good at what they did but found no time (in between winning awards) to look at the space in which their (high turnover) staff sat every day or to spend any time thinking of their agency's culture beyond that which was fabricated for the client. Quite frankly, why should they? If the agency is winning buckets of awards, you can attract top-notch talent easily, so why spend time nurturing the people you have or wasting precious money on a nice space

> **Decent music, pictures of people and places that remind me of great times, some proper coffee (I'm a serious coffee snob) and a sketchbook really get me in that place to start getting inspired.**

for the drones? I spent a year in this idea-generation hamster wheel, but it taught me some valuable lessons about how to deal with working in a space and an atmosphere that can be counterproductive to creativity.

At its heart, any good creative space should facilitate open, productive and collaborative work. The open-plan studio where people can wander around and freely chat about ideas is a great instigator of the "happy creative accidents" where one idea merges with another and becomes an even bigger one. Collaboration of thought produces bigger ideas and oils the wheels of innovation. You can't do this while working in a silo or by sitting all day staring at a brick wall with your headphones on. You have to be comfortable within your space.

The key to my creativity is being happy, and that's why I surround myself with things that make me smile. Says designer Ben Powell, "Decent music, pictures of people and places that remind me of great times, some proper coffee (I'm a serious coffee snob) and a sketchbook really get me in that place to start getting inspired." Ben Curzon ponders that the ideal creative space, "would probably be a perfectly climate-controlled, pure O2-filled, post-Walter Gropius designed bubble made entirely of curved touch screens, suspended by organic cotton from a cherry tree in the middle of the Lake District" but that the "reality is a bit of natural light, possibly a

— Ben Powell, designer

vintage film poster on the wall, but more likely a load of foam boards covered in Post-It notes with poor grammar. And that's fine."

"We don't go for exposed brick walls or an especially minimalist 'look at me I'm a designer' approach to the studio," explains Paul Davis of Overthrow Productions. "We just try to keep it comfortable and productive. There's some nice artwork we've collected on the walls and bookshelves of inspiration to dip into whenever you feel the need."

An element of personalization and, as Ben Powell notes, "things that make you smile" is evident in most creative spaces, such as vintage posters or artwork on the walls—anything that elevates the space away from being an "office" and transforms it into a studio. One agency, magneticNorth (known as mN to their friends), knows quite a lot about producing stunning creative work for clients such as the BBC, ARUP, Reuters, and Marketing Manchester. Based in a converted loft space, mN has struck a balance between a busy commercial enterprise and a space that has been developed organically by the staff who works there. When you arrive at magneticNorth, you enter the studio's library, a cavalcade of ephemera from all corners of the globe and from all eras over the last fifty years. The library is a working library, and there's a stamp that is used when books are taken out on loan.

# *Studio people: I'm not mad, I'm just not you*

**IN ANY SOCIAL** or working environment, we meet people who operate with a different set of mores. They've been brought up differently; they may like different things, have different tastes, have good or bad manners, be sensitive or not … You get the idea. They might come across to you as thoroughly bonkers, but what you have to remember is that you're coming across in the same way to them. They're not mad, bad, strange or peculiarly misguided … They're just not you. Understanding that in its basic form will help you deal with people you encounter during life. It's also a good principle to remember when dealing with fellow creatives or if you're up against the machinations of large (and not so large) corporate creative working.

## Creative directors (and executive creative directors)

When we think of great idea people, we tend to reflect on the golden days of advertising and cite people such as adman extraordinaire David Ogilvy or his contemporary John Hegarty as paragons of ideas, savvy businessmen and creative leaders. People to follow, respect and admire.

These days, and with rare exceptions, people seem less bombastic and showmanlike than the elder statesmen of the big idea. Creative directors are less prone to standing on tables and gesturing wildly with a maniacal glint in their eye. Quite frankly, this new digital creative side of things probably needs a few people like

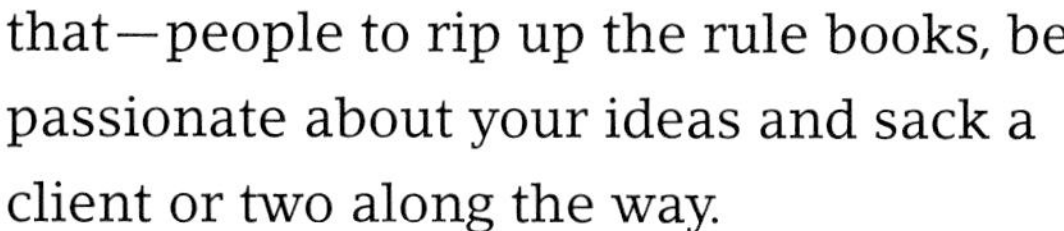

that—people to rip up the rule books, be passionate about your ideas and sack a client or two along the way.

Creative leaders should be colorful and never boring. How can they lead creative people by being dull? They should also know the tricks of the trade when it comes to being a social and political butterfly and have a naturally gregarious side. This is essential if they're going to bring in new work from leads or manage creatives' careers and mentor them successfully. The job is all about communication and understanding the business and a client's needs. It's not for shrinking violets.

## The holy grail of creative directors

If you haven't experienced butterflies in your stomach when presenting to a creative director, then you probably don't rate him highly enough to warrant them. The best creative director to work for should be a total pain in the rear at times but someone you admire and creatively rate highly. After all, if you're following the conventional route through a career, wouldn't you like to be in a similar position one day?

Creative directors should be great editors. They'll know just how much spice to add into a creative campaign without spoiling it. There is rhyme, reason and some technique to this, but it's also done to a large degree by instinct. You don't find the word *instinct* used on many project outlines. These documents are mostly concerned with the nuts and bolts of a project's delivery and are created to ensure it meets budget and its timeline. Instinct can't readily be

**Instinct can't readily be rationalized. It's an innate skill that we, as some of the cleverest animals, have buried, as we can't apply logic to it.**

rationalized. It's an innate skill that we, as some of the cleverest animals, have buried, as we can't apply logic to it. We're always told to create a rationale for our designs, but to write one of these and include the line "I did that because my gut instinct told me to" would be considered highly unprofessional and lacking in methodology—but you should listen to that little voice. Learn to trust it and let it take you on exploratory journeys while working on a project. A good creative director knows how to channel their little voice and has a feel for what will work.

If you ask a creative director to rationalize all their creative steps, most will admit to a degree of "swinging by the seat of their pants" style and "let's give it a go" gusto.

The big trick of the creative director's trade is to know when to listen to others. Good ideas gestate. The seeds are sown, and a combination of elements helps them grow. That combination is the team that the director trusts and listens to.

In any industry, many a manager of many a team will moan about individuals in it. Usually this is to make that manager appear busy or put upon or to cover some failing of their own: "Oh woe is me with the awful underperforming team. Oh woe. Oh woe... (repeat ad nauseam )." Any managing director worth their salt listening to this plight would point at that manager and say, "It's your team—you mentor them, you brief

them. It's your problem; go and fix it."

In creative, the buck really needs to stop with the creative director when it comes to how good the team is. Subscribing to blame culture can have disastrous effects on a creative's morale.

The creative director is there to shape, lead and protect the team and address any issues internally within that department. Running to the boss to tell tales after school only makes the creative director appear weak and unable to run a team effectively. It also makes him appear untrustworthy to his own team.

But of course creative directors are only human. They are influenced by all the factors and niggles of life that get to you. They will have their favorites on the team (the ones who get the best work given to them); they will have hangover days, moody days, nothing-going-right days and mocha whoppa frappuccino overcaffeinated days.

We'd like to think that people in positions of authority can remain cerebrally level throughout the day, but they're all impacted by external forces that affect how they give feedback on work, brief the team and generally perform their job. No one says the creative director has to be your best friend, but understanding the external factors affecting them can help you pick your moment when it comes to discussing a campaign, presenting work or asking for a holiday.

# Only work with friends if they truly hate you

**WHEN A GROUP** of friends form a working partnership, they have to learn to communicate on a different level than the social one they currently use. Working with friends in a collective or a start-up agency means you're working with people who know all your little foibles from the get-go. There's a fine line between love and hate, and if your friends love and support you enough, you can be sure they'll also hate you enough to speak their minds without having to rein in their views and opinions due to a need to be politically correct or to follow a set company process of feedback.

This is good and bad. If you welcome that type of directness, then you'll thrive in that environment, but at times a structured approach to dealing with feedback, opinion and the pressure of deadlines helps ensure that he who shouts loudest isn't the only one who is heard.

## Professional head space

There's an old adage that states you never truly know someone unless you live with them. Considering the amount of time spent during the working week together, this can also be applied to working with other people, and in particular, when working with friends it demands (for your own sanity) a clear division of responsibilities. This will help prevent problems arising from ego battles or ownership issues relating to projects or the way the business is run. Also think about having an independent advisor who you can turn to should you need business or project advice from someone with less of an emotional connection to the friends you're working with.

## Working towards becoming friends (again)

I've seen several successful friendship collectives fall apart after one member has taken umbrage at another's actions and they've stopped talking. There is no professional issue that can't be sorted out with a mediated discussion. If you have an open and honest dialogue during your professional relationship, then issues should be confronted and dealt with as they arise. Harboring animosity and letting it build up will eventually have it spilling out into a relationship-damaging torrent of anger. Say how you feel calmly and rationally, and if you can't do this, use an impartial mediator to help bridge the gap between you and your friends and co-workers.

## Due diligence

Pop-up friendships are those that occasionally happen on a big night out when you meet similar creatives and they become your instant best friends. This is not a lasting condition. In this state of creative bonhomie, don't agree to work with them. It's a mistake you'll only make once, as it can cost you time, money and your sanity in the long run. If you're working in a freelance crew (as I often do when taking on film projects), try and hire people who are recommended to you by people you trust in the industry. Failing that, perform due diligence on them, which is where you objectively look at their work histories and see if they're suitable to do the work at hand. Have they had previous experience with this type of work? Have they worked

> **There's something peculiar about human nature when working in a team of three, particularly if it's in a crew or team working remotely ... Somebody always becomes the third wheel.**

in a small team or crew before? Is there a genuine interest in the work? If the answer to any of those questions is no, then don't touch them with a barge pole, as you could be heading for a situation where you are carrying people who believe just turning up is enough and have a slapdash attitude towards the work at hand. Try and work with passionate people who feel the same way about creative, film, development, code or photography as you do.

### Three is (not always) the magic number

There's something peculiar about human nature when working in a team of three, particularly if it's in a crew or team working remotely. You'll find that at times two members of the team will bond, and this bond will alienate the third. Or two will bond over issues with the third, which in turn leads to (more) alienation for the third. Somebody always becomes the third wheel. This situation becomes worse when three become two and two become one and partner up or marry. One short film director tells me of having spent a summer working in a crew of three made up of two others who were hired without any due diligence and having to spend an infuriating few months finding them becoming increasingly difficult to work with. They'd become emotionally attached to each other by continually having issues with the work that they'd turned into their "common enemy" and something that they could emote about together. Eventually their issues became directed at a common enemy in the

form of the director himself, and before long, the smallest of tasks became insurmountable problems, with words continually turned into swords for them to throw themselves on.

> **Director:** "Would you mind awfully moving that lamp a little to the left, please?"
> **Crew:** "Move the lamp? Why do you hate me? Is this all I'm good for? This makes me so upset ... It's giving me pains in my tummy having to do this."

Having emotive issues over a person brings people closer together, especially those who are trying to become emotionally close. The third person could be the twenty-first-century equivalent of Mother Teresa and they would still be seen as the outsider or the one to have issues with. In this situation, if the director had done his homework (and due diligence), he would have learned that both individuals had never worked for any one person before. They'd only ever worked on their own projects, to their own deadlines and to the beat of their own drum—never before in a team where you have to be mutually supportive and adaptable within it. Working for someone else was always going to be a problem. In this situation, you can attempt to heal the rift or part company. After repeated attempts to solve the issue, the couple eventually vanished without trace to the Valleys, never to be heard from again.

A blessed relief most probably.

Due diligence can save an awful lot of problems with people later on.

# Agency speak: A translation guide for survival

*People rarely say what they mean, and it can be hard at times to understand exactly what they're trying to tell you. When receiving feedback from a senior creative, you may often feel like you're expected to be a mind reader. For example, "I don't mind it" means "It's pretty shit but it's okay," and if someone says the work is "interesting," they actually don't have an opinion at all. I was once told by an art director: "That reminds me I have to take the rubbish out when I get home." This sort of response means the person to whom you're presenting is a total pain in the rear and that what you've presented them with is very, very bad.*

You'll find you'll get a lot of this kind of obscure feedback. But don't just take it from me. Here are some favorites from other designers.

Jeitz

Annis

**“This is a great start,” means “This is absolutely not what I wanted, and can you start again, please?”**

– Caroline Annis

**“Can we try this?” actually means “I think my idea is way better and I’m going prove it to you.”**

– Franz Jeitz

**“I like it but I’m not sure about the color. Could we try it in blue?” means “I don’t like it but I don’t really know what I want and I know that I am not being much help. However, I know that I like blue; everyone likes blue.”**

– Caroline Annis

**““ASAP” or “There’s no fixed deadline,” are both code for “I needed this yesterday.””**

– Franz Jeitz

**“Agreed.” in relationship to a fee quote actually means “Sucker, we would have paid double.”**

– Franz Jeitz

# The Right Way to Use the Left Side of Your Brain

# *Inspiration: The story of Picle*

**IT'S AN UNSEASONABLY WARM DAY** in March and we find ourselves filming in the quintessentially English town of Broadstairs on the Kent coast.

"Did you know that Vikings didn't actually have horns on their helmets?" declares Three Men and a Camera's assistant producer Matt Holding. Sound designer Joe Luck and I groan in response. We're used to "Matt Facts," as they accompany us on most shoot days. The fourth person in our party is intrigued, however. Interaction designer Alex Harding is recording this throwaway bit of knowledge on his iPhone. Not by taking a photo, recording a sound or even with a video. He's preserving the moment with a "Picle."

*Picle inventor Alex Harding and Three Men and a Camera sound designer Joe Luck*

*Alex Harding is an interaction designer at Made by Many and the inventor of Picle. Picle is an iOS app which captures a sound bite with an image. It's been likened to "Instagram with sound."*

Alex works for **Made by Many** (http://madebymany.com/), an agency based in an old wharf building alongside the Regent's Canal in London. This former industrial working space is now occupied by twenty-first-century makers of apps, social products and networked services for the web and mobile. They do this for companies such as UK terrestrial broadcasters ITV and Channel 5, as well as Skype and British Airways.

Alex is the inventor of Picle, an iOS app that allows you to take a picture and record a sound at the same time. These individual Picles can then be put together as a story and played back together. It's a way of digitally pickling your memories. If you think back to those hazy childhood recollections, they're usually made up of a disjointed sequence of images and sounds rather than videolike sequences. There's a certain fascination with looking at still

*Alex had the inspiration for Picle during a bank holiday visit to the quirky little seaside town of Broadstairs on the English Kent coast. To tell the story for the 2012 South by Southwest festival in Austin, Texas, the film crew Three Men and a Camera took him back to Broadstairs to film his inspiration.*

images, and when they're combined with a "flavor" of that environment delivered as a sound, it makes the image much more powerful. If an image can speak a thousand words, then you're now more likely to hear them.

We're here on the beach in Broadstairs producing a short film about the inspiration behind Alex's invention. The following week will see a large cotillion of staff from Made by Many fly to Austin, Texas, for the annual South by Southwest (SXSW) conference, where the great and the good convene to discuss emerging technologies and new ideas. It's a hotbed for networking and innovative new products. Usually there's a spluttering of new apps released at SXSW all vying for feedback, love and favorable reviews. It's a tough audience to crack, and the event itself is under the auspices of the press, bloggers and voracious tweeters who will sneer, praise or be indifferent to a product in 140 characters or less.

Tim Malbon, one of the founding partners of Made by Many, summed up the buzz, hype and general four-day intoxication of SXSW to Relax In The Air (www.relaxintheair.com): "We like to bring a large group out with us and stay in a house together with the headspace to be completely immersed in what we do and indulge ourselves in that and hang around in the morning wearing underpants and really get to know each other."

Ahead of the underpants soiree, we're busy revisiting the origins of Alex's vision.

*Alex Harding, interaction designer at Made by Many, tries out Picle on the beach © Made by Many / Paul Wyatt 2012*

A public holiday in the summer of 2011 was the perfect time for a trip to Broadstairs for Alex and his girlfriend. A place that, thanks to the character and friendliness of its people and the quirky charm of its architecture and surroundings, would inspire Alex to develop something that would receive favorable write-ups by *Forbes* and *The New Yorker* and become the talk of South by Southwest.

"I went there with a glimmer of an idea of what I wanted to do," Alex remembers. "Instagram is the usual way I'd document a trip to the beach, but I wanted to try

something different this time. Broadstairs is a friendly place with great sounds and character to it, so I started to take pictures with my iPhone and then record a voice memo sound separately."

Alex spent the rest of the day taking pictures around Broadstairs. One of the places he visited was an antique shop full of records, toys, tapes and postcards—ephemera from the not-too-distant past now held up as antiques for the retro minded. "I bought a Beach Boys album, and the lady who owned the shop was talking continuously the whole time so I had to get a photo and record her talking so that I could remember exactly what it was like." The shop also sells postcards from as early as the turn of the twentieth century to the 1950s and 1960s, "snapshots in time" as the shopkeeper would refer to them. Alex wondered what these would sound like if they could have recorded a sound bite at the same time. How much more would the picture be able to tell us about that time?

"I didn't have the idea of stitching the sounds with the images until the end of the day," he says. "It was a few days later that I decided to make a prototype using Adobe After Effects to stitch the sound together with one image. After doing one, it made sense to stitch all the sounds with the

images and make a story of them about my trip to Broadstairs."

The result of this was a video called *Day Out at the Beach* (http://vimeo.com/23201420), which Alex used to illustrate his idea of "What would Instagram sound like?" in a blog post on the Made by Many website. "I hadn't done a blog post for the site before, so I was a bit worried, as there are some amazing posts up there about new technology, new ideas, happenings in the business; that type of thing." Alex took a

deep breath and blogged.

The blog post caught the imagination of readers and the team at Made by Many. "The reaction was positive and I'd in effect created a prototype of what the app became. We love building things at Made by Many, and I think that's really rubbed off with me. We always prototype and by having this After Effects-produced story of images and sounds, it proved easier to get people excited and on board with the project."

Made by Many don't make their own

> **“So you end up asking questions like, ‘How do you go about physically doing this thing of merging an image with a sound?’ Do you create a new file format?”**
>
> — Alex Harding

products. They have clients to keep happy on a daily basis so resources for their own work is minimal. However each year for SXSW they have a bit of fun by changing their company homepage into a “SXSW takeover,” and in 2011, they took along an iPad app called Holler Gram. This was an idea developed to amplify the back channel chatter that goes on behind the scenes at SXSW. So Holler Gram became the equivalent of a glowing sign where messages are displayed and held up and the app simultaneously tweeted the message into a hash tag stream—a radical departure from the way iPads are usually used at conferences. This willingness to be a bit cheeky and subversive paid off, with Holler Gram proving an unexpected hit. The bar was raised, and for SXSW 2012, Made by Many chose to develop Picle as a minimum viable product (a limited beta) for the event, the perfect place to test it out and have instant feedback.

The next steps were to put together a team to realize the potential of the prototype. “So you end up asking questions like, ‘How do you go about physically doing this thing of merging an image with a sound?’” explains Alex. “Do you create a new file format?”

iOS developer Julian James and Alex worked on several other smaller prototypes to test what worked best. Was it recording the sound at the same time as the image? Or should it be after the image has been taken? They decided to give the user the

option of both. Picles need a home, so the team created a web service where they could be uploaded and viewed by those using the app. The Made by Many way of working is very agile, with stand-up meetings and internal feedback being added into the build of the app and web service almost immediately.

"The team was never more than five people and this was all started only two weeks before SXSW," explains Alex.

When thirteen members of the Made by Many staff arrived in Austin for SXSW wearing Picle T-shirts, they got noticed. "People would come and talk to us about Picle, and we started to get lots of feedback via Twitter and blogs and reviews," says Alex. Indeed the reviews and tweets rolled in, with *Forbes* declaring in a headline "Picle takes SXSW" and going on to say that, "Adding sound to stills is one of those aggregative improvements that makes you face-palm yourself and wonder why it took somebody so long to do it just this way." *The New Yorker* remarked that, "Picle is to video what text messaging is to phone calls." Praise indeed.

"The feedback was great and the best moment was actually seeing someone using the app in the street," says Alex. "That was just brilliant, but the consensus was that we needed to include more sharing options. We'd always made this as a beta to test at SXSW so we could get this feedback, and it has proved invaluable."

The heady days of SXSW saw the app

gain forty thousand downloads in less than a week. "You come back from that and you have to take it in a slightly more serious way," Alex remarks. "We do more stand-up meetings and catch-ups every day now. The next steps are all about sharing and connecting with Facebook and Twitter. We're also looking at the option to export your Picle story as a video to share on Vimeo or YouTube."

Made by Many are probably the most reactive agency to feedback out there. They know the power of the end user and have a genuine desire to make things that are built well. If they made sewing machines, then they'd be Singers rather than some dodgy import with wonky needles. The team understands that they should build products that are almost co-built with the target audience in mind. The feedback from this audience is then fed back into the product. By doing this in a very ordered and fast way, they are able to create something that people are more likely to use and, most importantly, use again. This very open "bring the user feedback in right from the get-go" approach would appear most beneficial to making useful and interesting products. It's at odds with the very secretive approach adopted by some other app makers who, out of fear of a stolen idea, hold their cards so close to their chests that even they can't see them.

The next steps for a product that started life as a glimmer of inspiration in a seaside town in Kent look exciting. "We could put a feed within the app so you can see other people's stories and Picles," suggests Alex.

Picle was the talk of the town at South by Southwest with over 30,000 downloads and 20,000 plays of the video in a matter of days.

"There are some great things we can do with geo location so you could perhaps search for the sound of London or Austin and it would then merge people's Picles together that feature that sound. Even more exciting is how you could search for gigs or sporting events. Perhaps you could watch the Olympics 100 meters by people taking Picles?"

Picle is an example of a great bit of inspiration and an experiment in lean product innovation. It's available in the app store and it doesn't cost anything.

This brings me back to the video shoot for "The Story of Picle" (http://vimeo.com/38250876 ) on that balmy March day. I blame the sea air, but we've ended the shoot in a pub, the landlord of which is quite struck with the idea behind Picle, and Alex is gamely showing him how it works. "I see," says the landlord. "Memories not only with a picture but with a sound." We all

smile and nod approvingly. "But what about the money?" he continues. "You'll make a million from this app!" Alex replied that it wasn't about the money. It was all about giving people the opportunity to share their stories. I was so taken aback by the unabashed sincerity of what Alex had said that I'd unwittingly turned the video camera off. I certainly wasn't going to ask him to say it again, but I'd curse myself rotten on the train home for not having captured it the first time.

*Already downloaded the app?* LOG IN

# PICLE

Preserve the moments that matter. Telling stories with photos and sound clips.

THE STORY OF PICLE

For more information, check out our BLOG

BROUGHT TO YOU BY

MADE BY MANY

# Brief Insight

## ***Seven projects, seven approaches to creative solutions***

# Sponsorship bumpers for Discovery Channel/ Singapore Airlines

## The agency

**Why Not Associates**

## The project

A set of sponsorship bumpers for Discovery Channel, sponsored by Singapore Airlines (SIA). The original set was focused on the new Airbus A380, whereas the most recent set was used to highlight South East Asia destinations.

## The brief

The creative brief from the agency (JAM) was based on the idea of "transformation," and each spot had to include a moment of transformation that revealed the Airbus A380. Each different bumper was assigned a fact relating to the Airbus, and these facts were the basis for the imagery.

## Brief insight

We looked at the facts, which were largely statistically based and concerning scale, distance and measurements. This tied in nicely with the idea of flight path lines and diagrammatic illustrations. So we storyboarded each spot with this in mind—creating a look combining vector lines and pencil illustration with a strong color palette and typographic elements. The transformation idea was used to transition into the end shot of the Airbus, and this technique was kept consistent throughout all four spots.

## Working with the client

The scripts were already quite tight and defined, as the facts were researched by JAM. However, we were able to work with them to select four facts to proceed with.

5.5

same
height

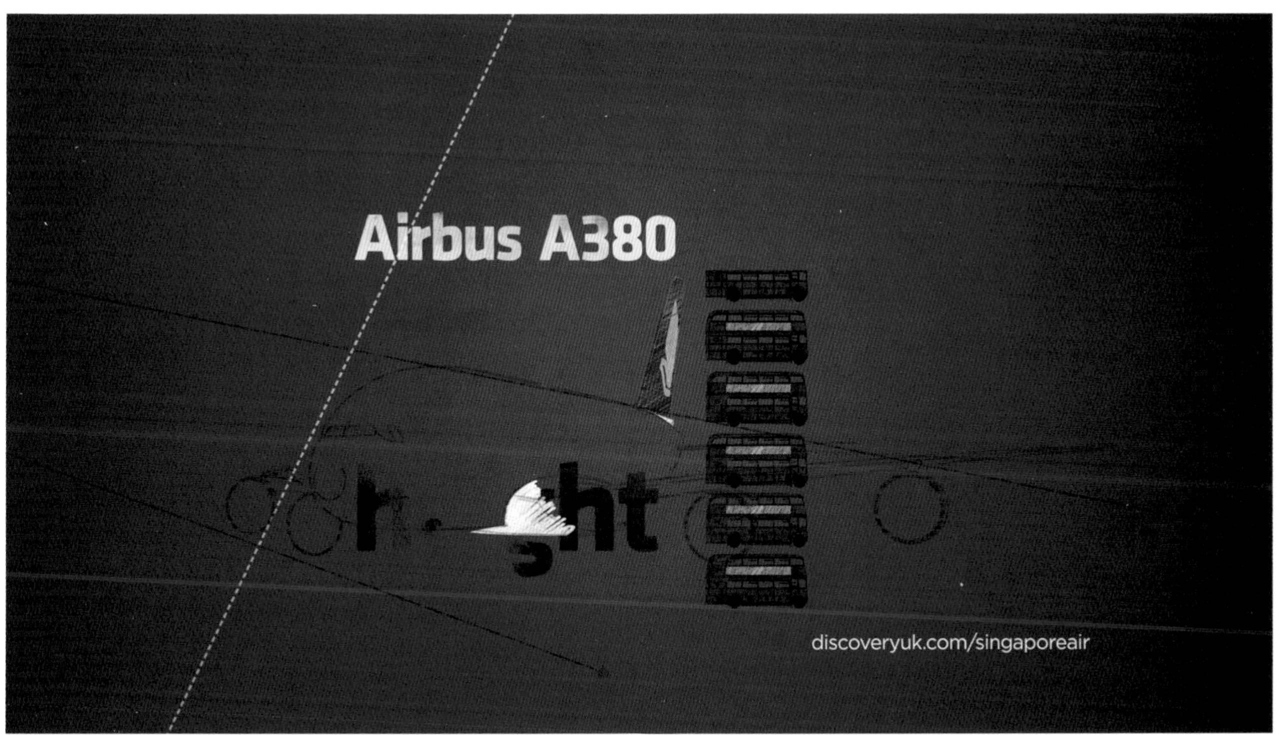


We chose the ones that seemed to lend themselves to a simple illustrative approach, and these happened to be the numerical/statistical facts.

This was the first project we worked on with JAM, and we have developed a good working relationship with them since.

Both the project manager and designer worked closely with the client. At Why Not Associates, we think it's very beneficial for the designer to talk to the client directly throughout the project, where the creative aspects are concerned. Not only does it save time (and e-mails) but it means that we can solve problems more efficiently. The project manager also deals with the client, overseeing the schedule and budget for the project.

## Concepts

The initial phases of this project ran quite smoothly, as we presented detailed storyboards for each spot prior to starting the animation. Originally we had a starker aesthetic, more relating to plans and diagrams, but this did not create enough distinction between each spot. We opted for a strong background color unique to each animation, which resulted in a much bolder and richer end product.

In terms of presenting work to the

client at various stages, we usually have a schedule with some predetermined dates for feedback—especially if there is a tight turnaround. We made sure that our storyboards were clear, as JAM had to present them to Discovery Channel without us. Once they were approved, we started animating and presented work in progress renders in a couple of stages. Inevitably, there was feedback and things changed along the way—not only from JAM but from Discovery Channel and Singapore Airlines. Thankfully, the majority of the feedback for this project related to the SIA and Discovery branding rather than the overall concept!

## Launch

The project was received very well and won a Promax Gold award at Promax Europe 2011. They played out on Discovery Channel for over a year, and everybody involved was so pleased that we are just finishing another set to be aired alongside them this year.

*Title: Discovery Channel / Singapore Airlines sponsorship idents, Client: JAM Creative / Discovery UK Creative Agency & Discovery Channel, Design and animation: Why Not Associates, Year: 2011*

# *Whale Trail iOS app*

Ustwo co-founder and creative director Mills discusses the process for creating the popular Whale Trail game, and shares his thoughts on the creative process.

*Whale Trail is the highly addictive iOS and Android game produced with love and devotion by Ustwo in London's Shoreditch. Since it's launch on Android in January 2012, it has been downloaded over 20,000 times with an average 4.5 star Google Play rating.*

## People may think ideas are easy to come up with, but it's rarely true. How hard was it to "give birth" to Whale Trail?

Whale Trail was a natural progression; it didn't all come at once, but bits got attached to the initial idea, things got taken away and you just work and work and work until it all comes together. Anyone can come up with an idea, but it only takes one little, often silly, idea (like a flying whale) to start a snowball of ideas adding to the initial idea. More often than not, a joke idea is the one you go with because you can add more silly ideas to it and it works. We are proof that you can shine shit; we've had some success with lesser apps, but with Whale Trail, we struck gold.

## What type of creative director would you say you are?

I let the team get on with their jobs, I don't

do their jobs, and they don't do mine. I am the product owner. But we hire the best team who you can trust to work the best they can to make the best for you.

### *What's wrong with the creative industry at the moment? What are we not doing enough of?*

Overall, there are not enough risk takers. We started doing jobs for clients, and of course that's the safest bet, but when you become more established then you can try something new (in our case we invested in our own project, Whale Trail), focusing on creative products more than creating something for someone else. Companies need to hybrid up; eventually we want to become 50/50 in turnover, half from our own products and half from clients.

### *How do you get the best from your team?*

We hire people we know we can trust to work and do the best they can, and we know these people because they are the most passionate about what they do.

### *How do you keep your team motivated?*

Really the team we have are able to motivate themselves. When they are involved in making a campaign, if and when that project becomes successful, then they should be egged on to make more success.

### *Is it all about work for you or passion?*

Unquestionably it's passion. If this is just

a job to you and you're just in it to make money, you're in the wrong business—it's all about passion. With passion, you're not afraid to try new things, discover new techniques that can lead to new ideas and new concepts, and even if these don't lead to a final product, you still tried and you enjoyed it and you learned from it. Passion all the way.

### *You're a digital obsessive; is that important to be successful? To live, breathe and sleep digital?*

In today's society where everything changes so quickly and technology that we use or could use is constantly updating and re-energizing, I'd say it's very important to be obsessed or keen on digital. I use a lot of my spare time reading up on new technologies that can be useful to me and my company.

### *Specialist or generalist—which is best for this business?*

I think that when you're a specialist, you get caught up in your field and you miss out on what else you could be doing, but at the same time, you could be the best there is within that medium. If you're a generalist, there's nothing to stop you from being the best in one field while still excelling and learning and working with other fields.

### *Who is your hero?*

At the start of my career it would have been people who I learned from and inspired me, style-based companies. But now I'd say my hero is my father; he's the one who helped kick-start the business and always is there for support.

## Early concept sketches show characters and game zones

regular clouds
slow you
ice clouds
really slow you/
drop some trail
storm clouds
electrocute you/
drop most of trail

## Character development

## A vast array of characters were created for the game

## Whale and icon design concepts

WILLOW

## The various zones players discover on their journey

**... and what a fantastic journey it is!**

## Filming the music video to the Whale Trail soundtrack *(written and performed by Gruff Rhys)*

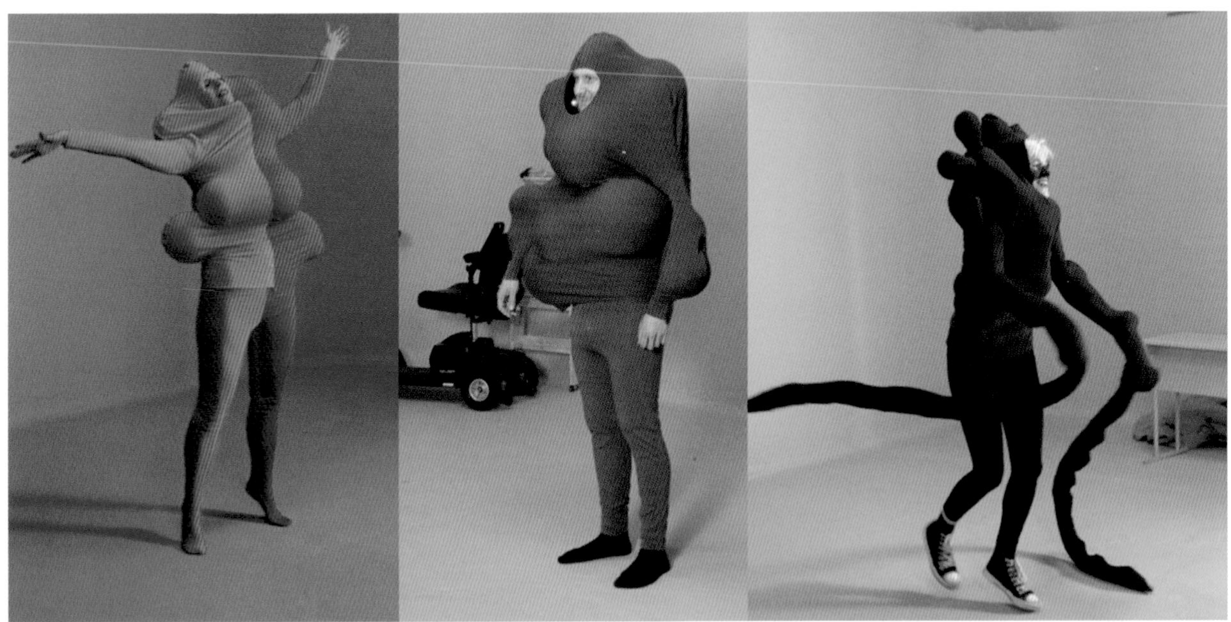

## Completed screens from the final game

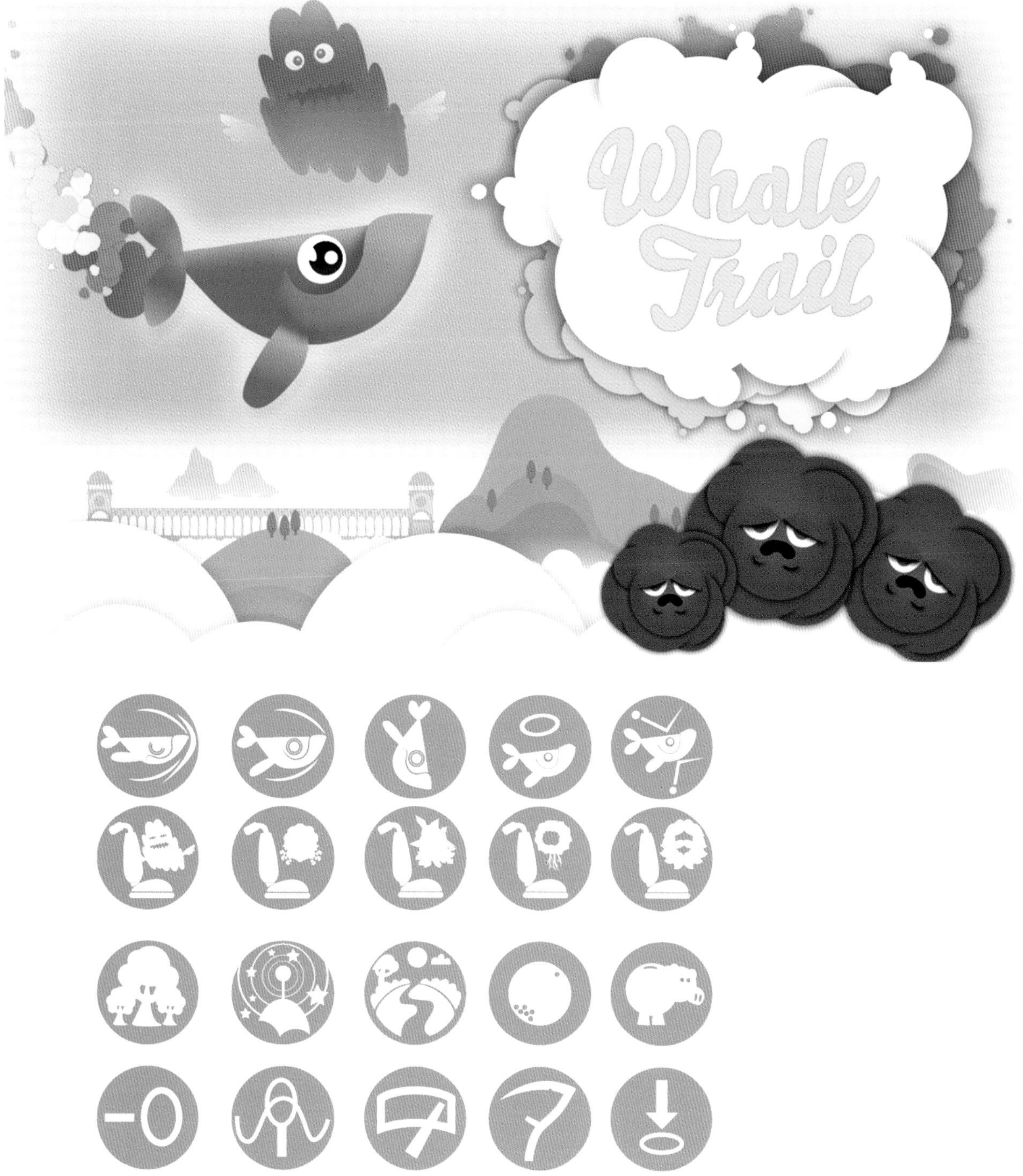

## The completed screens as they appear on a device

24x
412,177

16x
285,632
Frenzy
+1600

# *Desert Island Discs website*

Digital design company magneticNorth explains their innovative work done for BBC Radio 4's Desert Island Discs website from project inception to launch.

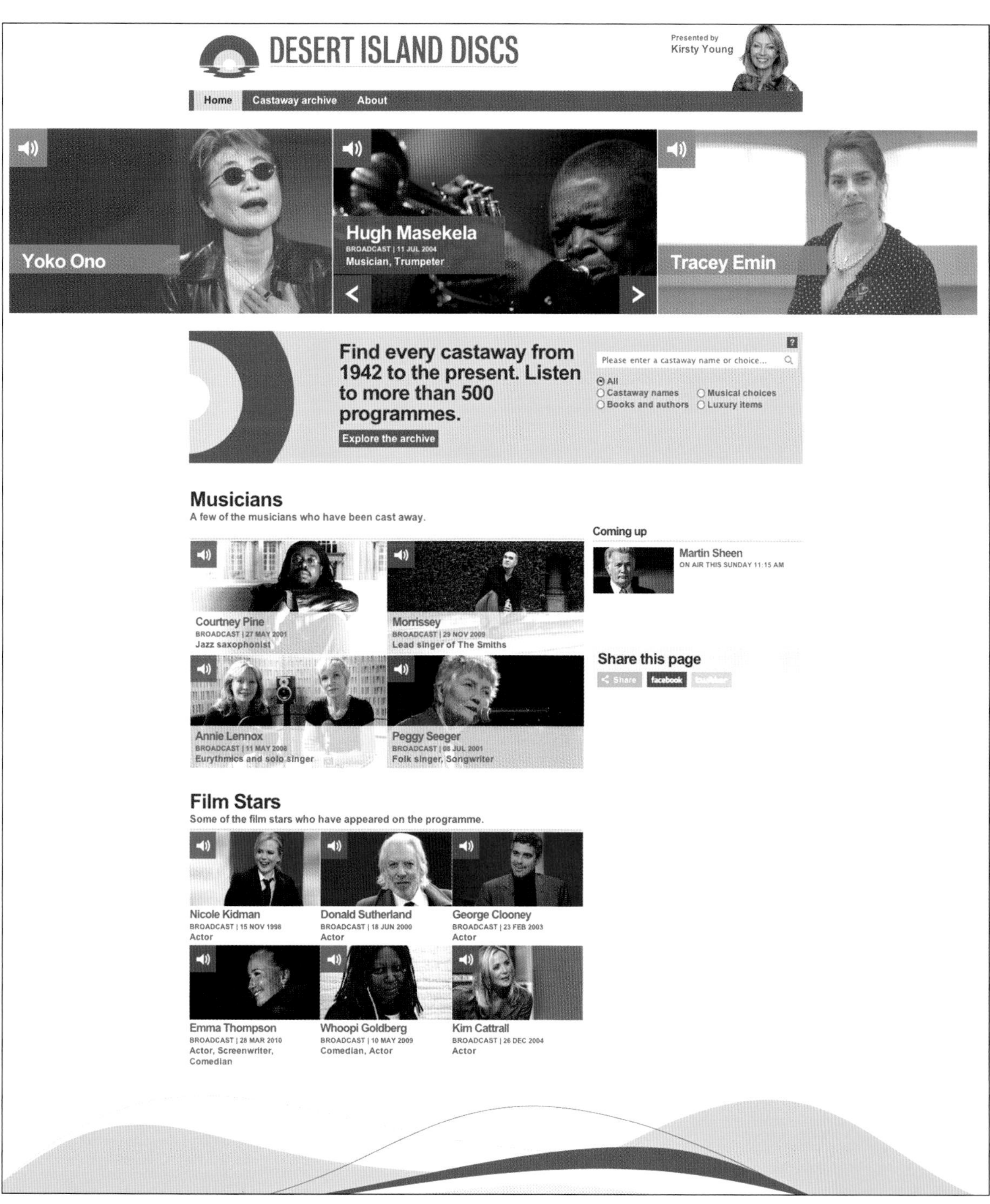


*BBC Radio 4's Desert Island Discs website was commissioned to house the program's vast audio archive, along with details of each desert island choice made by every guest since 1942.*

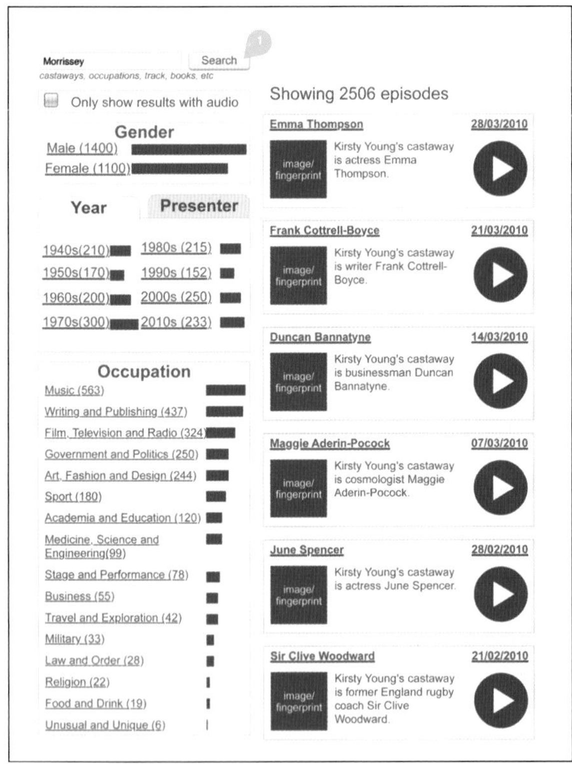


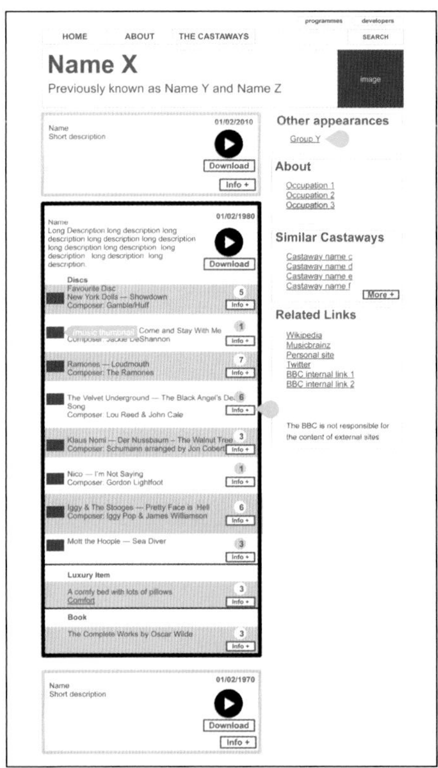


*Initial wireframing studies for the Desert Island Discs website drawn up before work in Photoshop took place.*

## The agency

**magneticNorth** (or mN to our friends) is a digital design company based in Manchester, UK. Established in 2000, we're a team of thirty digital thinkers, designers and makers creating commissioned client work for a selection of the world's most interesting brands.

We do all things digital, from websites and apps to installations. We love prototyping and exploring new platforms with our clients who include the BBC, ARUP, Reuters and Marketing Manchester.

## The project

BBC Radio 4's Desert Island Discs website (www.bbc.co.uk/radio4/desertislanddiscs) was commissioned to house the program's vast audio archive, along with details of each desert island choice made by every guest since 1942. There have been nearly three thousand guests, so you can imagine the volume of content there was sitting in the archive!

The site needed to be more than a static filing cabinet for seventy years worth of facts. The BBC wanted people to explore

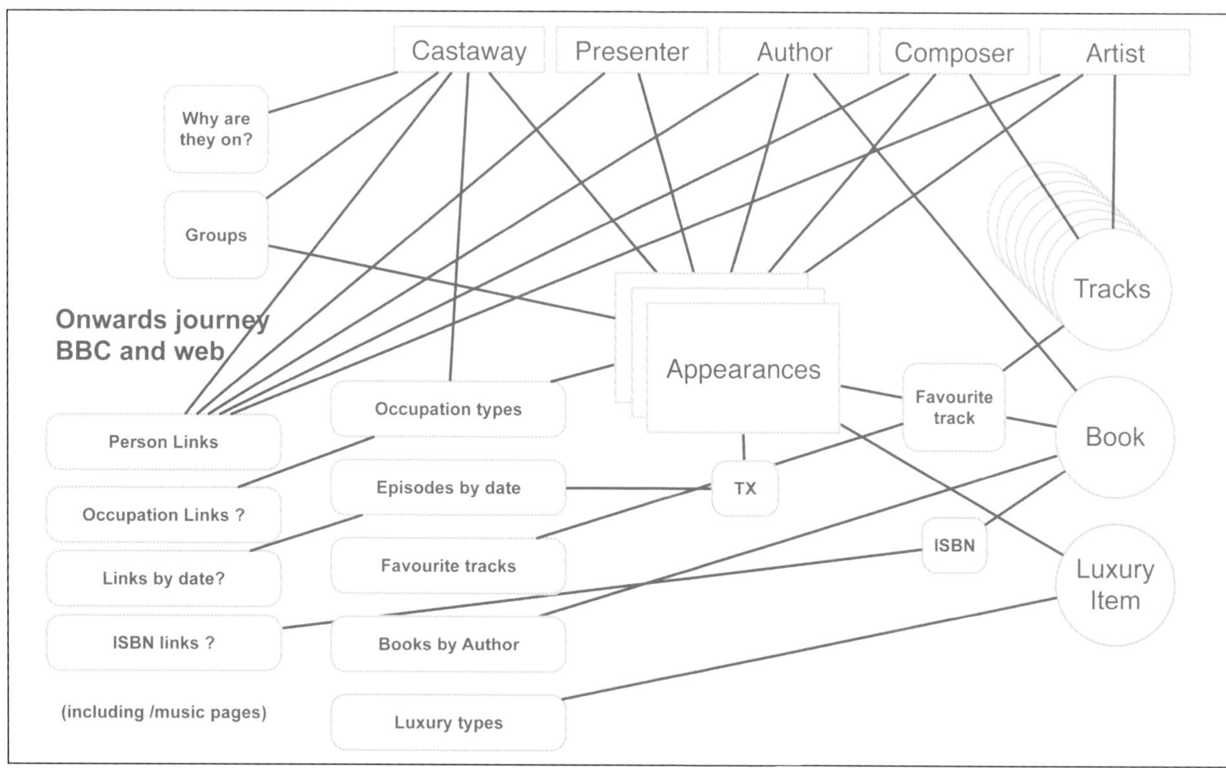


*The data model for the site*

and make links across the program's rich archive. They wanted us to create an enjoyable experience for users, so the audio and data needed to be searchable in a way that was straightforward and engaging.

The website was designed and developed by magneticNorth in conjunction with a BBC team spread across editorial, technical, design and production.

## The brief

The BBC had an ambition to create a major digital proposition for Desert Island Discs. The program holds a unique place in British popular culture, with an archive of enormous cultural value. A flagship website was needed that would make all the archive programs available. Targeted at a broad, mainstream audience, it needed to engage people who already love the program and encourage new audiences to discover Desert Island Discs through the web.

## Brief insight

We recognized a unique opportunity to redefine the role and impact of digital in

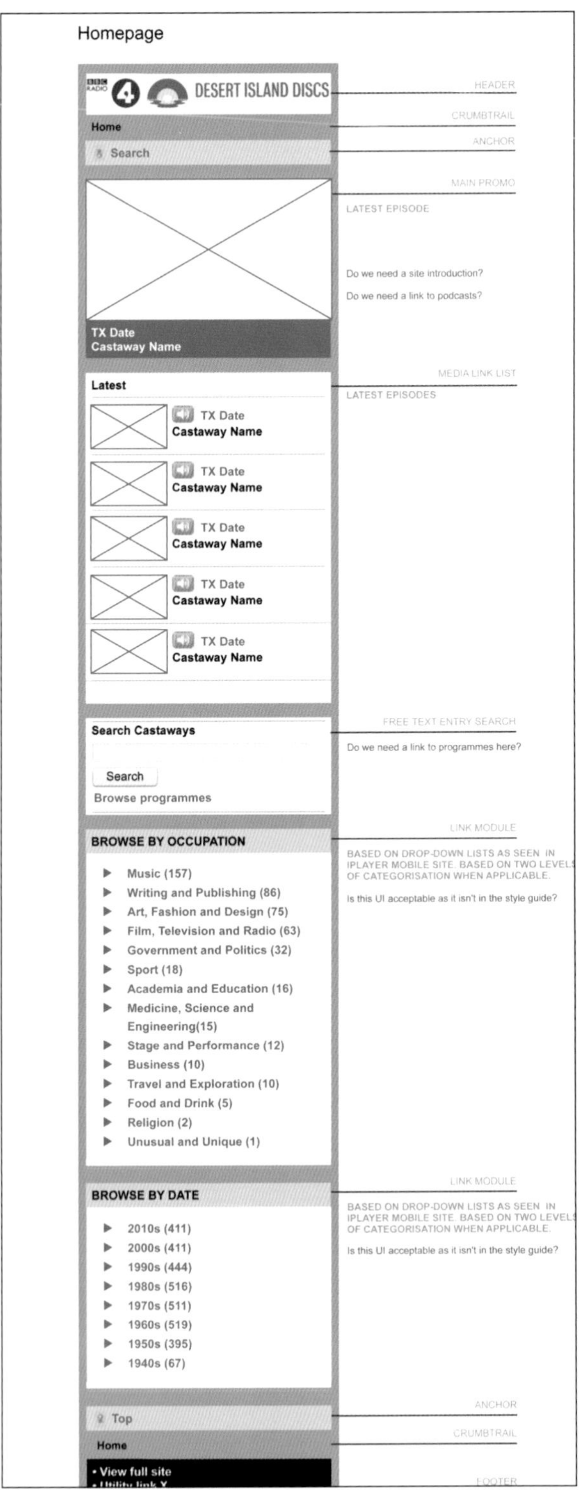


Mobile wireframe visuals

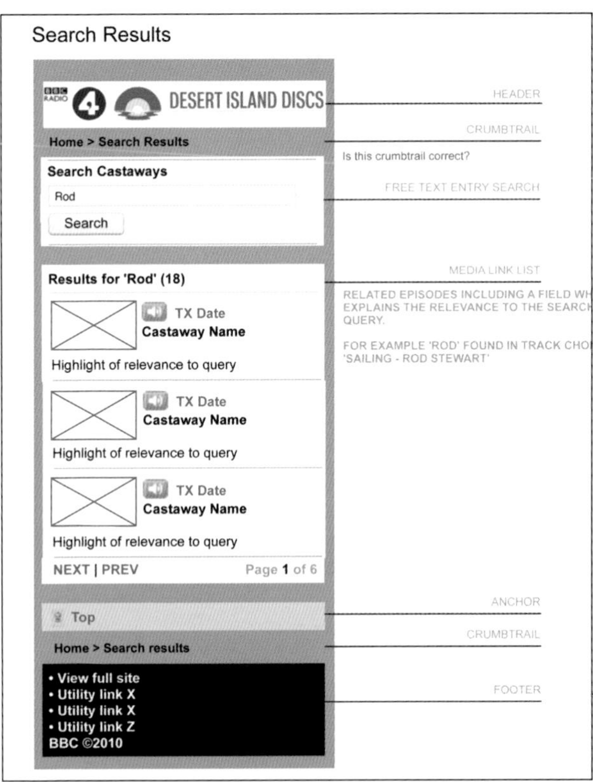


the Desert Island Discs brief—to generate a new level of audience engagement for the program. The thinking we developed, that won the pitch and eventually became the core concept of the site, was based around an elegant search and browse.

The brief was all about finding things; what was needed was a solution that encouraged curiosity and promoted serendipity. We proposed a solution that allowed people to search and browse the archive by the various facets of the available data using filters. So, for example, it would be easy to discover what female

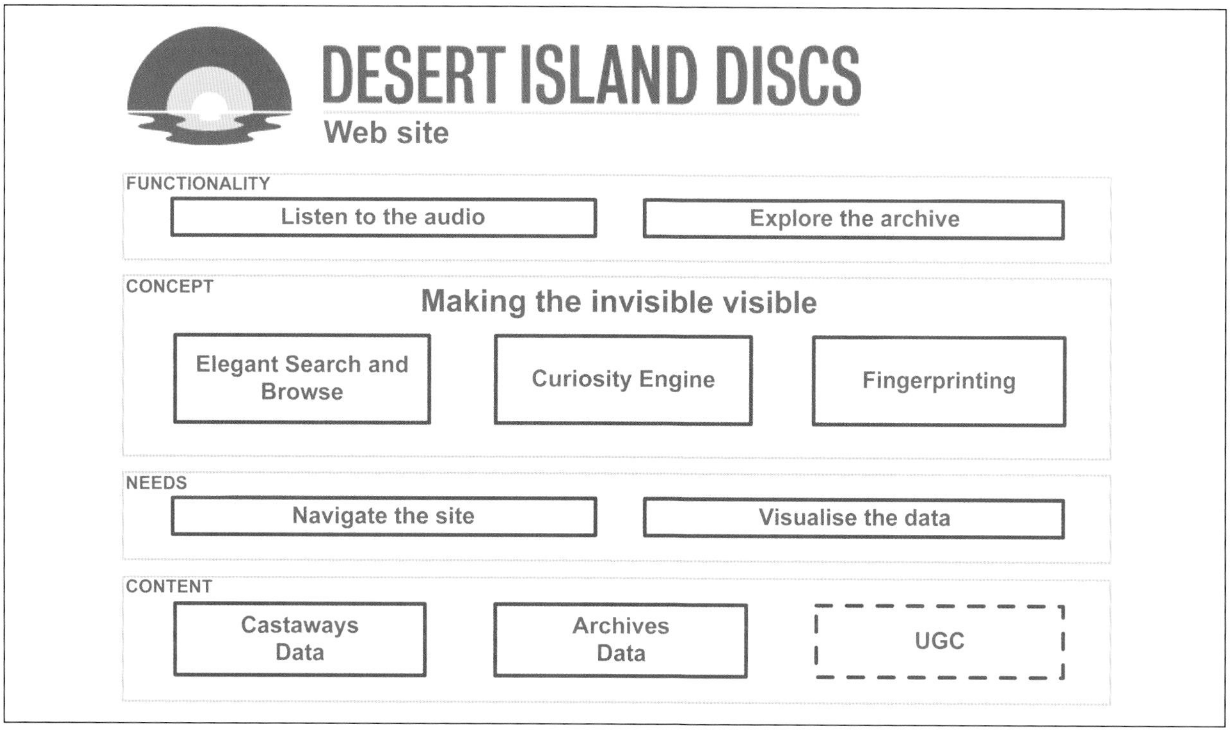

DESERT ISLAND DISCS
Web site

FUNCTIONALITY
Listen to the audio
Explore the archive

CONCEPT
Making the invisible visible
Elegant Search and Browse
Curiosity Engine
Fingerprinting

NEEDS
Navigate the site
Visualise the data

CONTENT
Castaways Data
Archives Data
UGC

*This diagram illustrates the proposed homepage function for the site.*

artists or designers have appeared on the program. Around this core concept, we proposed a robust technical solution, strong visual style and an interface that was fit for purpose.

## Working with the client

We worked very closely with the full client team throughout the course of this project, from the project kickoff, interaction design, design development and technical build. Both mN and the BBC value the benefits of working collaboratively to achieve the best results possible.

Communication was key to keeping the project goals and objectives in line with the original brief—through working sessions, tightly managed approval processes and regular status updates.

We quickly established a great relationship with the client team and worked together as a partnership. All mN's projects are led by a producer, as the main point of contact for both external and internal teams. Each member of the team is involved in all stages, and clients have access to everyone on the team.

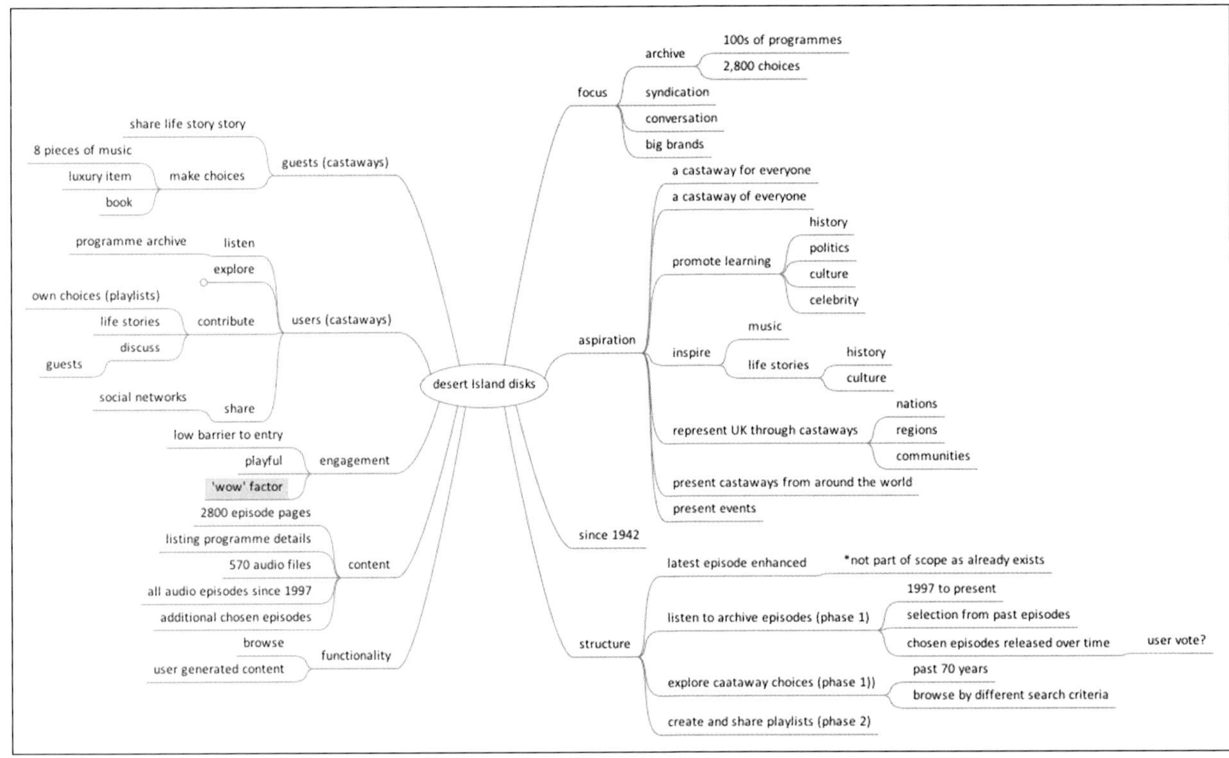


*This mind map represents the project wishlist*

## Concepts

The concept behind this website was "making the invisible visible." The site aims to transform the ephemeral nature of radio into a permanent visual representation. But this website does more than simply visualize a database. Like the program itself, it tells fascinating stories. It throws up unexpected connections between guests' choices and reveals some surprising selections.

In the early stages of the project, concepts were developed as a mix of sketches, wireframes and visual designs. These were discussed in workshops and iterated upon. The language used in the website for instructions and "calls to action" was extremely important to the project. The wording was incorporated into visualizations and tested in usability sessions. Various elements of the interface had to be prototyped, such as filtering and the display of results, allowing us to test our user-interface designs and the validity of the available data.

## Launch

The site launched to public and industry acclaim in April 2011. It has become a

An early prototype

much-loved destination for audiences—including those who already loved the program and others who have discovered it through the web. Between April 2011 and January 2012, 7.8 million archive episodes were downloaded.

The interaction design has had minor updates as a result of user feedback, and the site has been used to promote several campaigns, most recently to celebrate the seventieth anniversary of the program. We are extremely pleased with the site, and it sits proudly in our portfolio.

A behind-the-scenes look at planning

Celebrity chef Heston Blumenthal's castaway page

*The search function needed to be straightforward and engaging*

## Desert Island Discs Testimonials

"The website is amazing ... really amazing ... You can look at this website and feel a connection." *(Mark Ellen, Editor, The Word: Podcast, 3 June 2011)*

"Desert Island Discs: Archive Addiction… Curse you, Radio 4!... I must stop, it's eight in the evening and I haven't had breakfast yet." *(Qwerty, Pause Live Action blog)*

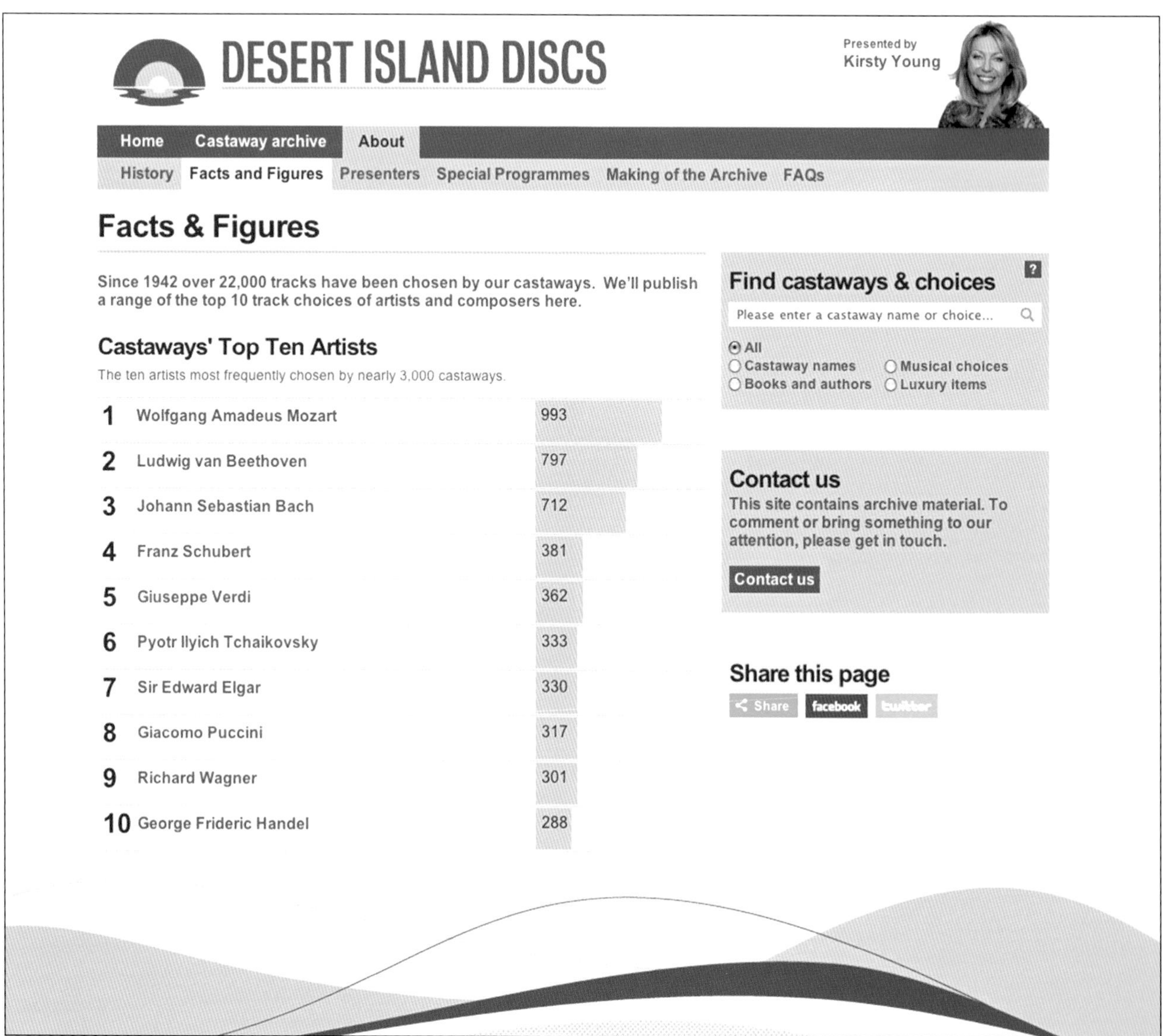


*Facts and figures*

"One of the most addictive and worthwhile music-related sites on the web" *(Chris Salmon, The Guardian, 30 September 2011)*

"A brilliant snapshot of our culture" *(@theokk)*

# An interview with magneticNorth Creative Director Adam Todd

**How do you feel when a brief comes in?**

Generally when a brief comes in, the adrenaline starts going, as you have a new chance to prove yourself and your team. You do get some sleepless nights, and sometimes it's quite daunting. It's exciting to do new work, though, and to understand the problems you'll have to overcome.

**How do you get the best from a team when collaborating?**

We try and keep the sessions light. We do have massive sessions at times but find that if you have everyone brought together for too long you lose focus. We tend to start with the essence of the problem at hand and pose questions; we then disperse and reform and see what the members of the team have come up with.

**Where do the ideas come from?**

Ideas can come from anywhere. When creating the archive website for Desert Island Discs, we got a lot of ideas from listening to the radio, as it was a related field. We try not to use the Internet til the past point; it's a fallback for us for ideas. We say there's no such thing as a bad idea, and the team has learned not to hold back on ideas because one part of an idea might work well with another. That's how ideas come about. You can get ideas at anytime: You might be cooking or running and come up with a fantastic idea for a campaign … then you just have to remember it. Coming up with the ideas is the hard bit. We read literature about ideas and techniques. When we have sessions, anything comes to the table; there are "no bad ideas," and we create an atmosphere where it's easier to put out ideas. Ideas rarely come fully formed; they develop into the final solution. It's important not to keep ideas to yourself because it's silly. You need to share them; this is how ideas develop. It gives the opportunity to put ideas out there to build on.

**What do you think of the industry habits of self-mythologizing?**

I believe you're only as good as the last project you produce. Not churning out projects less than the standard you set yourself. Desert Island Discs is a distant thing; we've since worked with more media and projects.

We've moved away from just building websites. Desert Island was the last website we've done; it was a website built with a website view. You work different ways with projects for Smart TV, or tablets. You should always be judged on your output.

**Does the creative industry make things look easy for the outside world and does that de-value what we do?**

In this industry, simplicity is king. The next generation of media users and makers are making things simple; easy-to-use things work better, sell better. But what people don't realize is how hard you have to work to make something simple. With Desert Island Discs, we had so many technical difficulties; results came back we didn't want. But the user doesn't know or care; they just want a project that works. They don't know the development and research that goes in, when things work and go well, when things are lost. They do, however, notice when things go wrong; that sticks out like a sore thumb. They see the final product, so it definitely looks easy for the user.

**How do you creatively steer a campaign?**

Communication is the main thing that steers a campaign. As we're based in Manchester and were working with the BBC in London, we had to travel back and forth weekly, and between the visits we would have conference calls and nonstop e-mails to frustrating levels. In the office, too, we would have many face-to-face meetings and planning sessions. When people go into the creative industry, a lot dream of working from home and having a few conference calls, but there's nothing like being with people where you're able to make decisions earlier. E-mails can get misinterpreted and [when you're face to face] you can easily discuss budgets and deadlines without waiting to hear from different people at different times. When you're dealing with the tech side, and finishing up "odds & sods," it's easier to do in a room of people rather than through a chain of e-mails.

**How painful was it for you to bring life to this campaign? Were there blood, sweat and tears shed?**

Plenty. Lots of technical issues we had to overcome. We were making a multifaceted navigation system, showing all episodes from the 1950s that could be filtered by years, names, professions. The implementation of this and the technology available proved more difficult than developing the idea. We pulled plenty of all-nighters and had to get new technology, as lots of people would be using it.

# *Valor # vInspired*

Tom Harding, interaction designer at Made by Many, discusses producing the innovative vInspired app for Valor.

*Thinking about volunteering? However and whenever you want to make a difference, the vInspired app produced by Made by Many helps you give something back.*

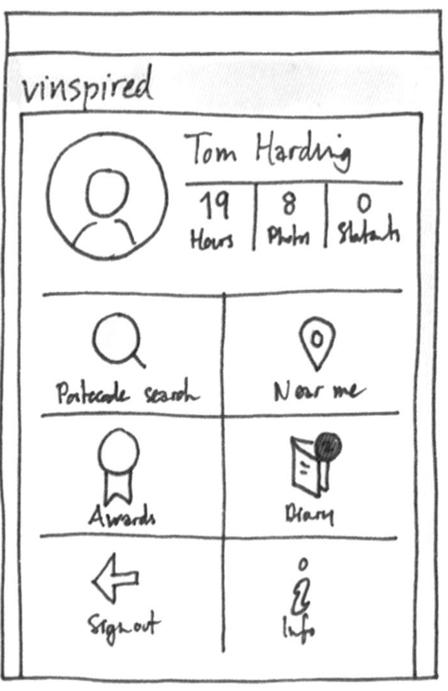


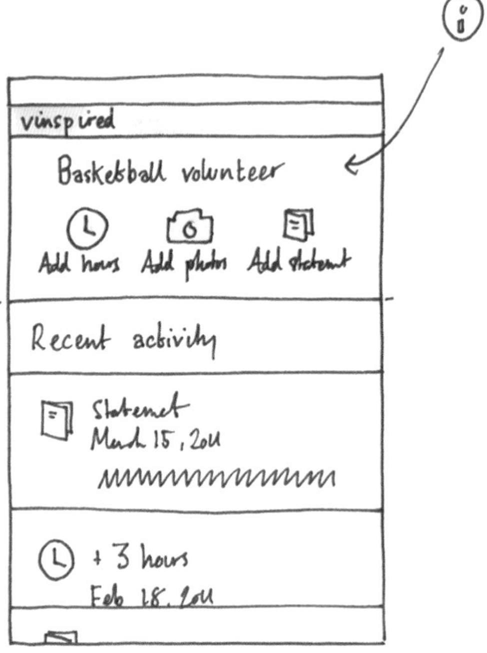


*Early sketches helped visualize the project.*

**vINSPIRED IS A MARKETPLACE OF** volunteering opportunities for 14 to 25 year olds.

As with all projects I work on at Made by Many, vInspired was a collaborative effort that I learned a huge amount on.

The team consisted of me, a service designer, a strategist who's also the partner, a creative technologist and a small team of developers.

We worked closely with the client, volunteers and partners to figure out how to create this volunteering service. My role as the designer changed throughout the project, but in the early stages, I visualized the complexities of service through simple sketches.

Once a direction was agreed upon, we set out to build a prototype to validate the service with users. The idea was to launch small, get feedback, iterate and slowly build a successful service.

This approach was new to me, and I found it really liberating. In the past, I'd assumed

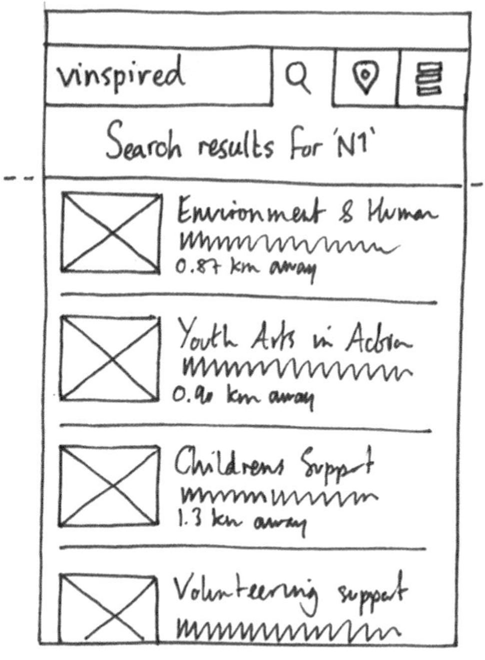
vinspired
Search results for 'N1'
Environment & Human
0.87 km away
Youth Arts in Action
0.90 km away
Childrens Support
1.3 km away
Volunteering support

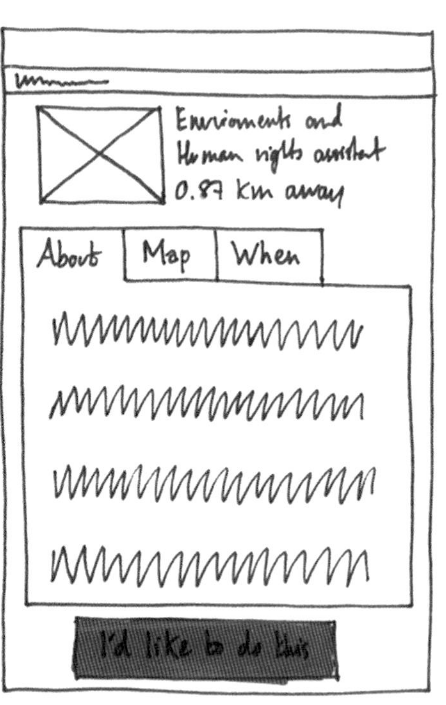
Environments and Human rights assistant
0.87 km away
About
Map
When
I'd like to do this

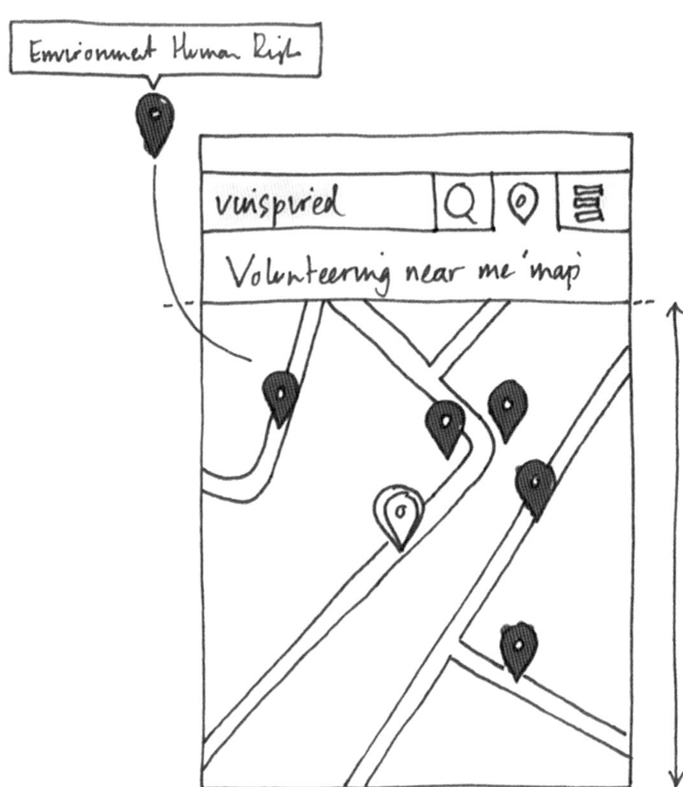
Environment Human Right
vinspired
Volunteering near me 'map'

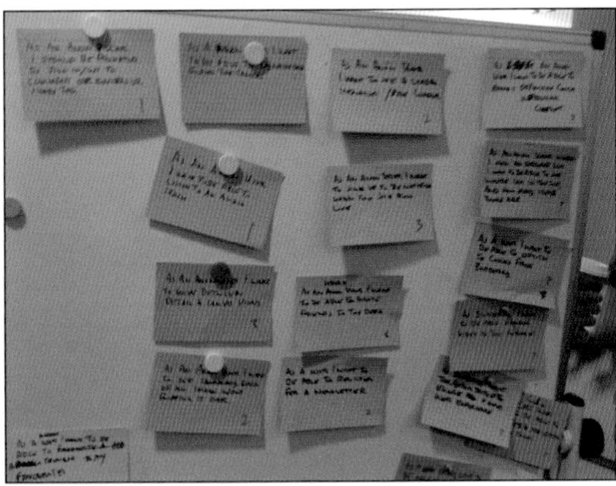

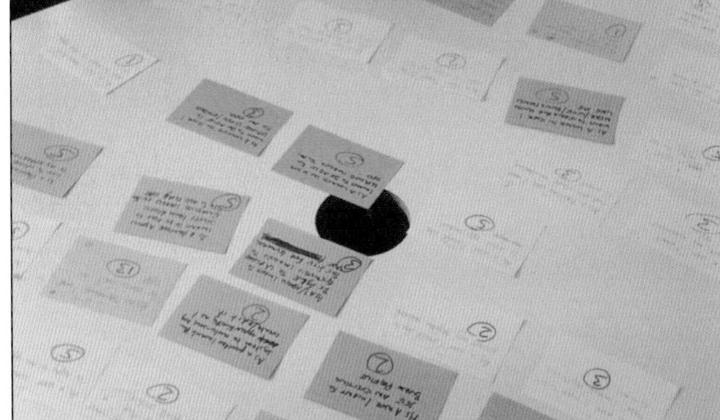

*Planning for the project was a collaborative effort.*

that I had to get a design perfect the first time because I'd only get one shot at it. This new agile approach was all about learning, making and testing until you get it right.

There are over one million volunteering opportunities from around five hundred different charity organizations available on the service.

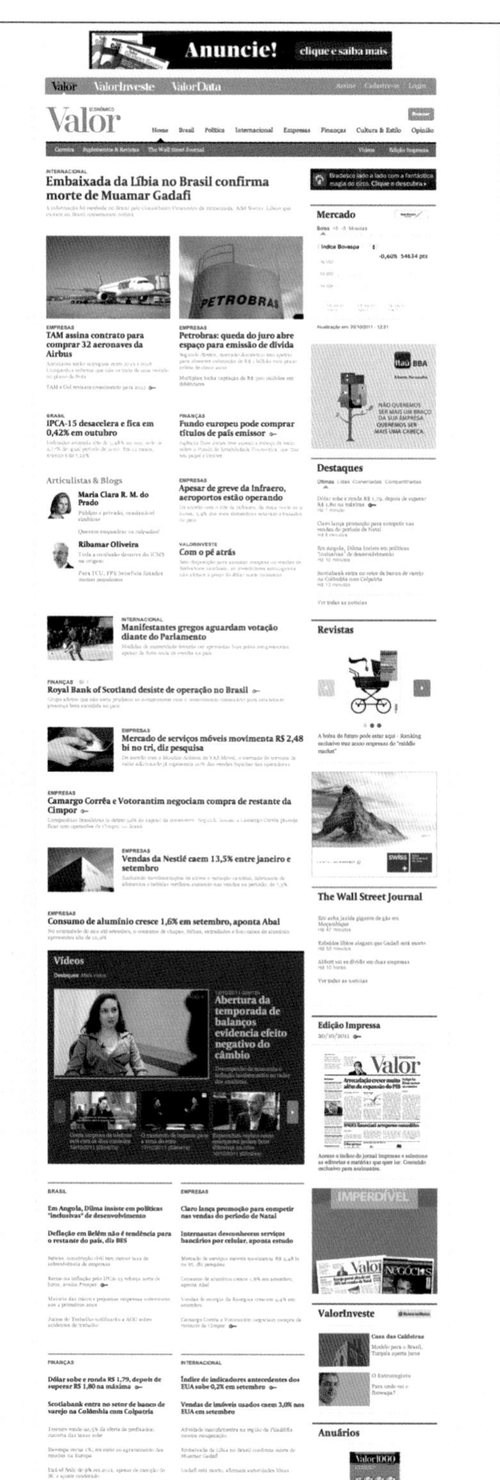

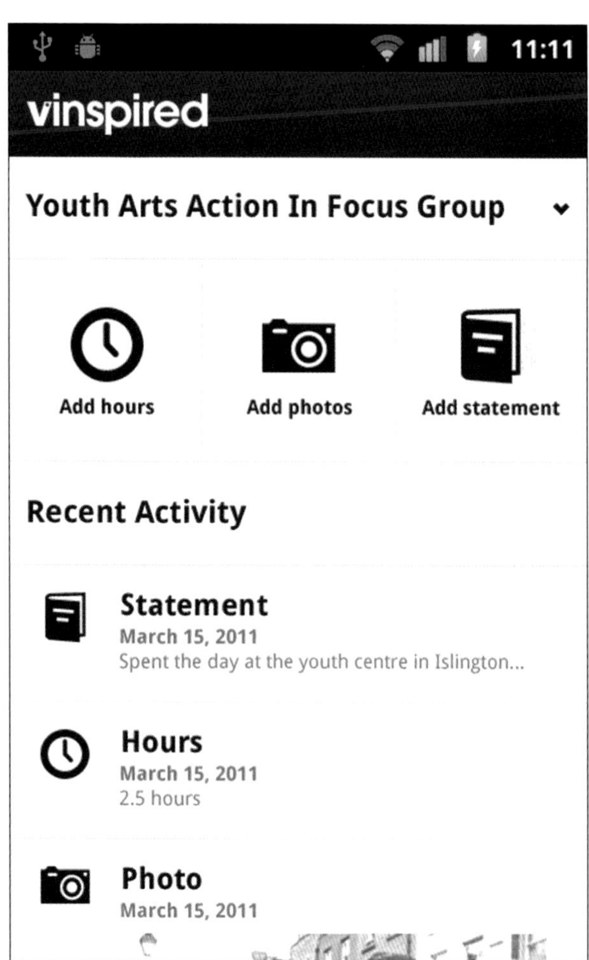


*The vInspired app shown here alongside Valor landing pages*

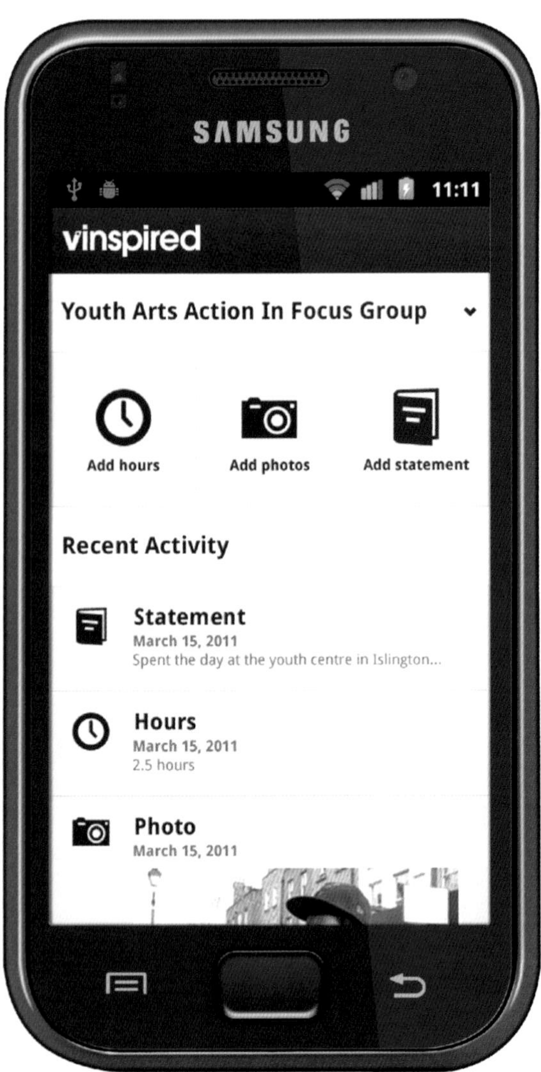


One of the most exciting parts of the project for me was recently designing a vInspired Android app.

The cliché is that good design is something you expect to find on iOS, but that Android apps are functional at best, or fundamentally ugly at worst. I disagree. We had a great time creating this app. An early prototype followed the iOS design much more closely, and while we gained a lot of useful code that made it into production, it was crystal clear that we'd need to do a lot of work to make it feel like a proper Android app, while still being easy to use and clearly part of the vInspired family of sites and apps.

We wanted an app that felt like it was created for your particular phone. As smartphone users, we've all experienced the frustration that comes with an all-devices HTML app that doesn't use native buttons, and we didn't want to put v's users through that.

SAMSUNG
11:11
vinspired
Youth Arts Action In Focus Group
About
Map
When
The 1A Centre, 1A Rosebery Centre, London, EC1R 4SR
I'd like to do this

02:29 PM
Back
vinspired
Volunteering for The Who Ca...
Discover
Record
Awards

BlackBerry
Find Your Opportunity
Enter your postcode
Find opportunities near me

## *Just Rosie*

Danny Whitfield explains that with an entrepreneurial project management style, he helped to produce a stylistically different spin-off of the world's longest-running soap opera — *Coronation Street. Just Rosie* began as an online special with a website campaign and Twitter and Facebook integration. The reaction was so positive that this online show was eventually premiered on television.

*This spin-off show from the highly popular ITV drama serial* Coronation Street *showed character Rosie Webster's journey from the North of England to London... on her way to discover fame and fortune.*

***CORONATION STREET*** **IS THE WORLD'S** longest-running soap and Britain's most popular TV show. We wanted to extend its much-loved storylines online through a unique adventure of one of its favorite young characters, Rosie Webster.

*Just Rosie* is an online drama that follows Rosie's trip to London, where she pursues her dream of becoming a famous top model. She'll do anything to become famous and ends up fighting with another model on live TV. The fight goes viral and her dream comes true, to some extent, when she's interviewed by real British stars of TV and radio.

We created a fun entry point into Rosie's world with a website that feels like she's made it herself, www.itv.com/coronationstreet/justrosie/showreel-and-tv/, and you can win prizes by entering competitions.

Basically, we wanted to build the content in stages, as more and more people were spreading the word amongst their friends, and it was important for us to make her biggest fans feel like they've earned the right to have content first—just for them.

The most innovative aspect of this project is that we have been able to begin a storyline in the main *Coronation Street* series and draw fans toward a brand new drama and adventure, thus extending its reach and entertainment, particularly with a younger

and more engaged (digitally) audience. We took the story across not only different platforms but also different ITV properties. So, you got to see how Rosie's adventure led her onto *Loose Women* and *Lorraine*. Because of this we, were able to serve and market the event across a bigger fanbase and extend the fiction into people's lives where they'd least expect it.

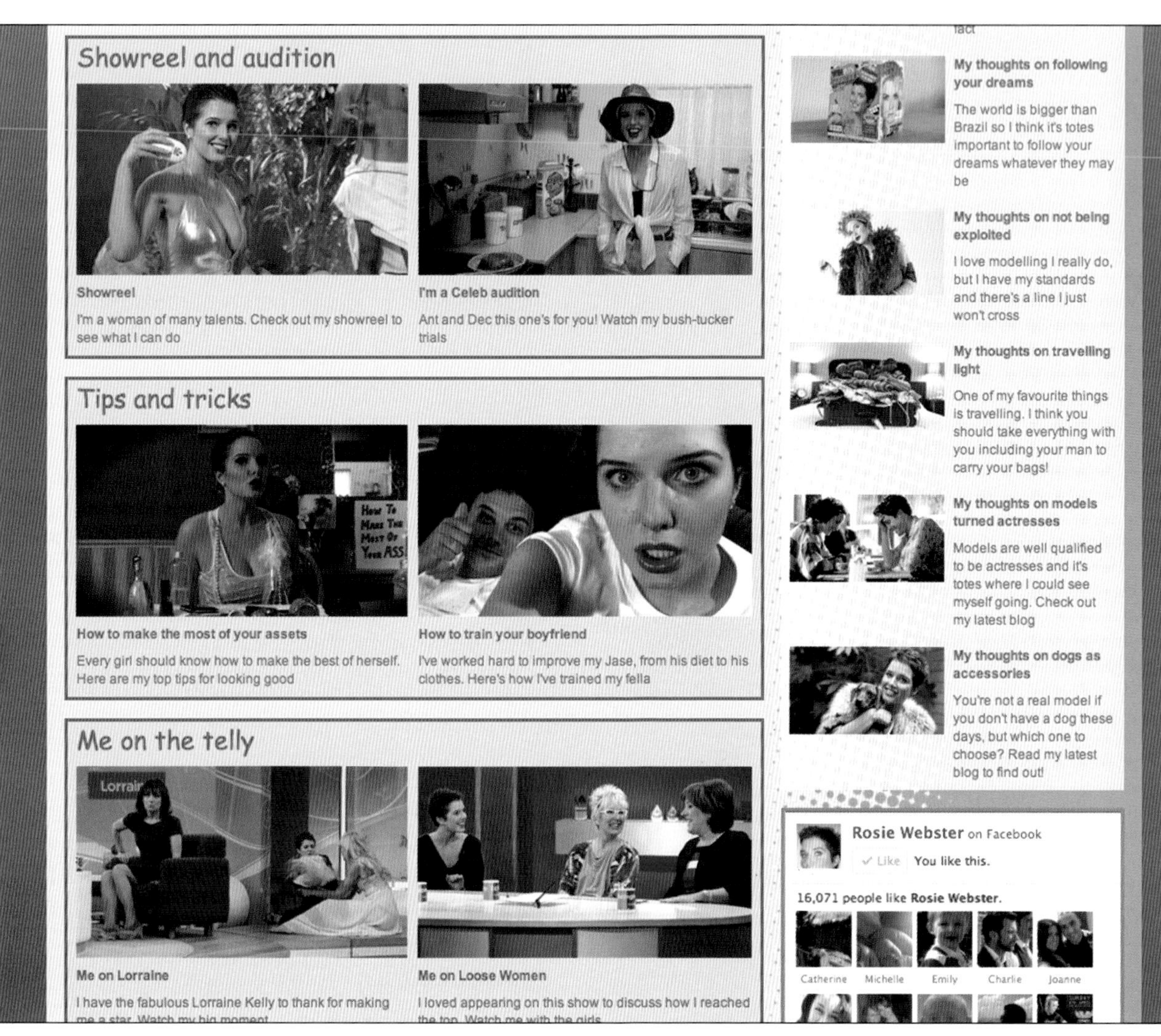


Also differently from any *Coronation Street* episode, we used a very creative editing and music style across the drama and cut between very short scenes to give it a high fashion/music feel that is much more exciting than the main soap.

We drove people across different platforms with this project by using Twitter, Facebook, websites, ITV shows, ITV2 and iTunes. One of its biggest successes that made people feel part of the action was the way "Rosie" (our dedicated digital script writers) could interact with fans not only via Facebook with extra storyline information but also through "Ask Rosie" on her website, which offered advice around audience "problems" inspired by her blogs. … We also were able to set up competitions to win "the hat" as featured on *Lorraine*, which is the cause of many of Rosie's problems.

THE
LONDON
STUDIOS
POST
itv

CINEMA

## *Just Rosie* also features a title sequence created using Adobe Flash and After Effects. Danny Whitfield and animator Tom Baker explain how this was created and the ideas behind it.

***It's unusual for shows to have title sequences nowadays—especially such distinctive, tone-full ones like* Just Rosie. *Was "setting a tone" one of your main reasons for commissioning the animation?***

**Danny Whitfield:** Yes, totally. *Coronation Street* is so well known that I wanted to find a way to quickly create a different tone—an alternative that was more focused on the individual character of Rosie. It was more about telling the audience familiar with continuous soap stories that this was going to be a complete journey told from beginning to end. Its other purpose was to let an audience who would have largely come from being a fan of the show to still get a sense of the familiar with the chimney pots and such like.

***Can you give us an overview of how you worked with Tom? What the original ideas were, what were the mandatory requirements and brand message?***

**Danny Whitfield:** The big idea was basically to show Rosie rising above the chimney pots of the rainy north and landing amongst the bright lights of London. The only piece of design we had to go on was a Rosie Webster business card made by the *Coronation Street* design team, which had some wings around her name …

I think I had originally said I wanted the

wings flying in to deliver the different letters of the cast and Rosie's name, but Tom created the animatic that basically turned the wings into Rosie—much better.

The requirements were about length of time—I wanted to fit in the main actors and writer, didn't have the time to credit myself and to also blend into the first short of the film, where the camera moves past the pink strips and rises up to meet Rosie.

**Tom Baker:** The concept came to me in the first meeting I had with Danny. I generally bring along a sketch book and try to flesh something out right away, as good ideas are often the first ones. Taking the strong imagery associated with the *Coronation Street* title credits (namely the rooftops), the *Just Rosie* titles would then leave the grey of Manchester, whoosh skyward, past clouds and planes and then settle back down on the glamorous skyline of the capital city. The budget was pretty tight at £500. I needed to basically get thirty-second title credits approved, signed off, and delivered within three or four days. If I could get any sort of message across describing the show as well, even better.

Despite the short time frame, I still managed to create an animatic (which Danny approved) and some stills. Once I had the thumbs up, I could finish off the titles and deliver the final version.

Initial reaction was so positive I was given a bit more budget (£250), allowing me to add a few more embellishments (rain, more buildings and more detailed animation) to create a very decent set of credits.

# Animatics

*Tom Baker animated the opening title sequence for* Just Rosie. *Here's the initial animatic produced to test out the sequence both for visuals and timing.*

## Finished Animation

*Stills from the completed* Just Rosie *title sequence. Produced by Tom Baker using Adobe Flash and After Effects.*

# Microsoft Surface Experience

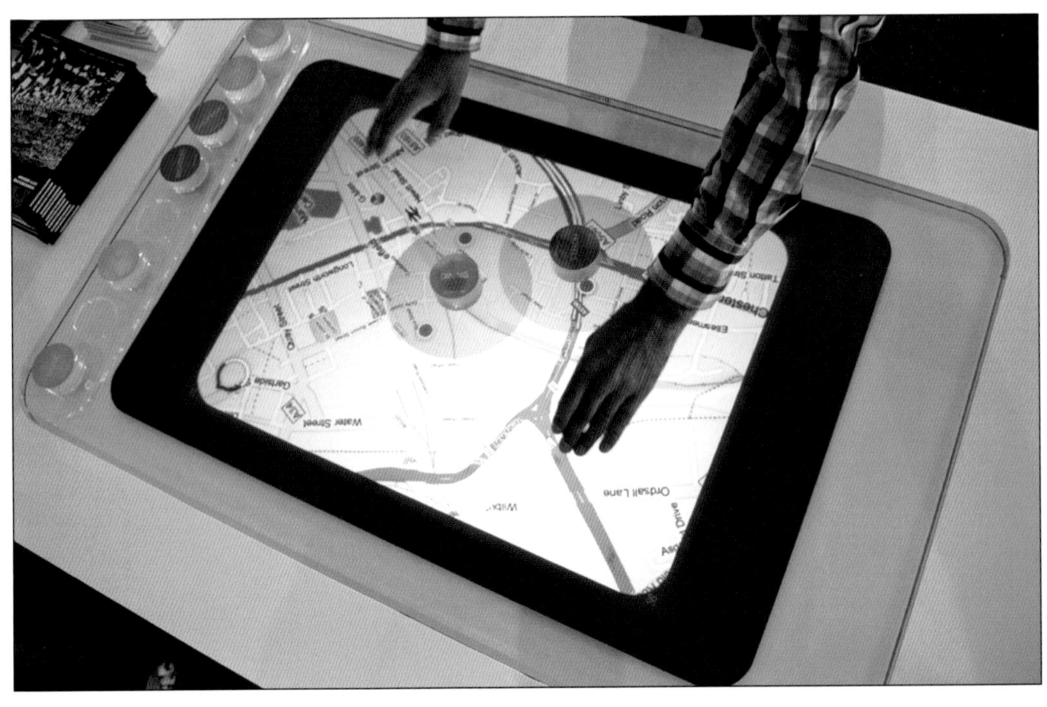


*magneticNorth created a unique interactive experience for the Visitor Information Center opened by Marketing Manchester in September 2010.*

## The agency

**magneticNorth**

## The project

A Microsoft Surface experience that formed the centerpiece of the new Visitor Information Center situated in the Manchester city center

## The brief

Marketing Manchester tasked mN with creating an application for their Microsoft Surface Tables that would generate a buzz around the new Manchester city center, by offering visitors something that was both innovative and helpful. mN had already created a Manchester API, known as FABRIC, and believed the Surface Tables would provide a playful new interface for this data. For the team at mN, the natural form this could take was an interactive map.

"We needed to be able to provide lots of useful information about the city," explains creative director Adam Todd. "Where the restaurants and clubs are; hotels, shops and tourist attractions. The solution would also need to be able to give people directions to and between locations."

## Brief insight

When approaching the design of the application, the first consideration was context: The space at the Visitor Information Center is about being useful to the people who enter it, so everything contained within the space needed to have utility as the primary consideration. The interactions had to be natural, the visual design tied in to the "original modern" design of the Visitor's Center.

With this in mind, the team at mN first started by researching the capabilities

> **“ We didn’t want people to feel intimidated by the technology but wanted them to feel free to touch and paw away at the tables.**
>
> – Adam Todd, creative director, magneticNorth

of the tables, playing with the installed demonstrations and reading Microsoft’s User Experience Guidelines.

“We really liked that the tables have the ability to recognize objects placed onto them. Pretty swiftly we hit on the idea of using objects to represent categories of locations across the city center. It was decided that we would have eight ‘objects’ that represented a section of Manchester life people might want to explore on the map. These include hotels, museums and galleries, nightlife, shopping and dining,” explains Todd.

Objects can be dropped on the surface of the table to trigger different categories, such as hotels, or a “what’s on” guide. By turning the object clockwise, the visitor can widen the radius to increase the amount of information shown on the table. They can select a certain event, look at the associated times, read a description of the venue and show any related costs. Any information collated during their searches on the Surface Table maps is then printable for free.

## Concepts

Designing for a Surface Table was very much a different proposition than designing for most everything else. The screen can be viewed from any angle, and up to forty people can be using it at any one time. mN found that static designs and wireframes had to be judged on the table itself to be properly tested.

The build of the application was iterative, with transitions and interactions tweaked to make the best experience. mN went through five rapid phases of development and, at each point, the client gave input on the progress.

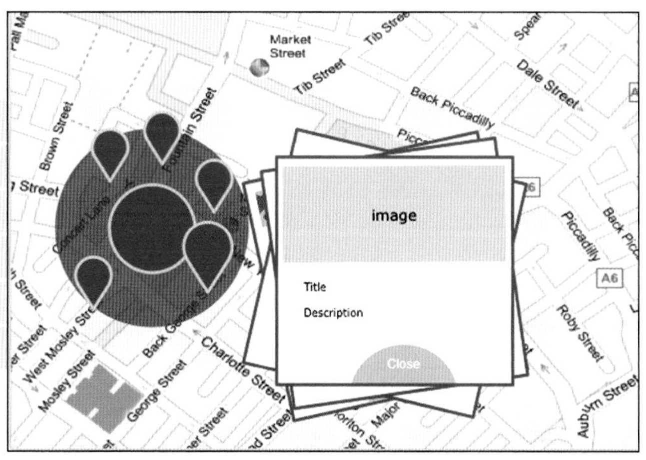
Market Street
Tib Street
Dale Street
Back Piccadilly
Brown Street
Fountain Street
Concert Lane
image
Title
Description
Close
A6
Piccadilly
Roby Street
Charlotte Street
West Mosley Street
Mosley Street
George Street

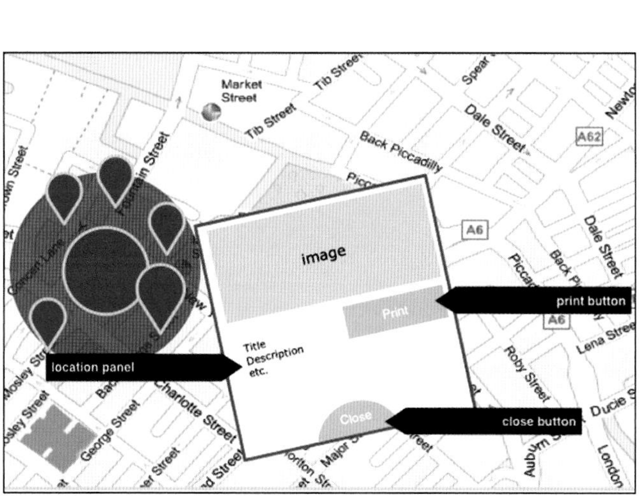
Market Street
Tib Street
Dale Street
Back Piccadilly
A62
A6
Concert Lane
image
Print
print button
Title
Description
etc.
location panel
Close
close button
Roby Street
Lena Street
Charlotte Street
George Street

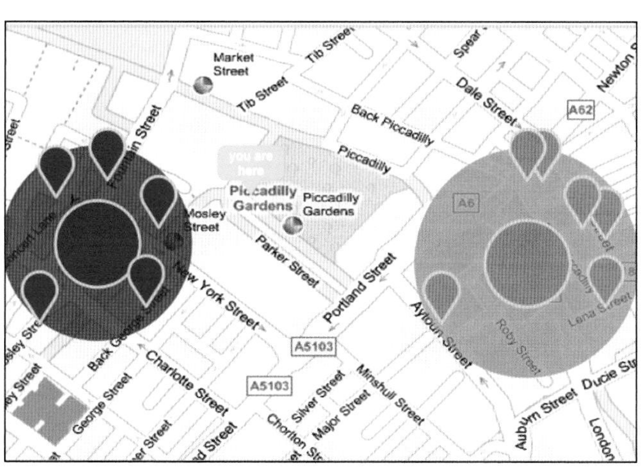
Market Street
Tib Street
Dale Street
Back Piccadilly
A62
Piccadilly
you are here
Piccadilly Gardens
Piccadilly Gardens
Mosley Street
Parker Street
Portland Street
New York Street
A5103
A5103
Charlotte Street
George Street
Silver Street
Minshull Street
Major Street
Aytoun Street
A6
Roby Street
Lena Street

HOTELS
NIGHTLIFE

## Working with the client

"This was our second project with the Marketing Manchester team, and so we knew they liked to work in a collaborative way as we always do," explains Todd. "Our creative team worked closely with Andrew Stokes, the CEO of Marketing Manchester, and his team to create a piece that would not only be a talking point but something actually used by people every day. We didn't want people to feel intimidated by the technology but wanted them to feel free to touch and paw away at the tables."

## Launch

"The reaction to the project was incredible," explains Todd. "Visitors to the new center were delighted and intrigued by the Surface experience, and there was great joy in watching people of all ages 'playing' on them. We often used to walk by and stand by the door just to watch people using them. In hindsight, we probably looked like total weirdos, but it was interesting watching both individuals and massive groups of boisterous school kids spend time with them."

"It was also great to see how the staff in the Visitor's Center, many of whom had worked in the old one for ages, easily adapted to using the Surface Tables to show people where things were in the city. They stopped using maps and pieces of paper as much; to us it was so important that the staff there loved the Surface Tables as much as the visitors would."

In its first year, the Visitor's Center saw a huge number of people interacting with the Surface experience, and it was hailed as a "best in class" Surface project by Microsoft. mN then began to work on phase two of the project, which added in route planner information. There are further iterations of the project coming in the future, with plans for further data sources to be added.

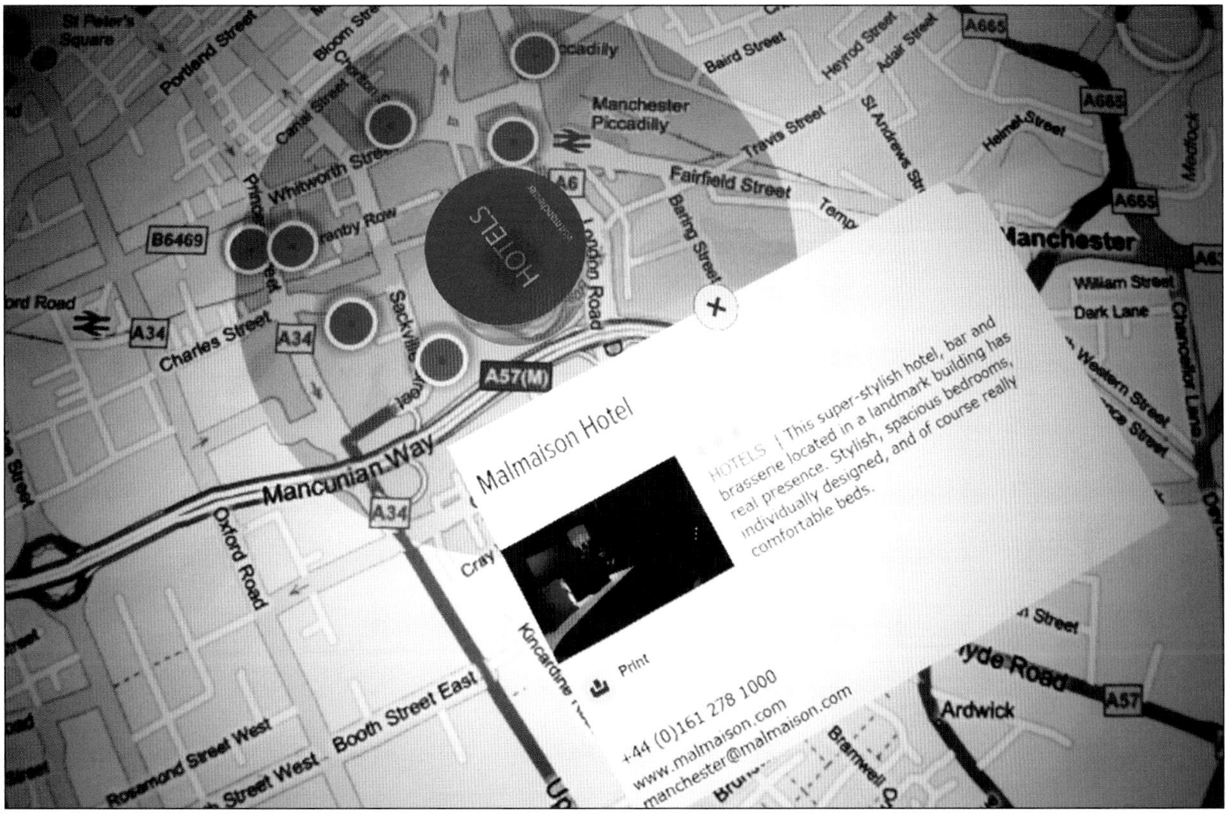

DINING
HOTELS
YOU
St Peter's
Charlotte Street
Portland Street
Mount Street
Longworth Street
Bloom Street
Chorlton Street
Canal Street
Whitworth Street
Aytoun Street
Central

# The War Horse Journey

*DreamWorks Pictures'* War Horse, *director Steven Spielberg's epic adventure, is a tale of loyalty, hope and tenacity set against a sweeping canvas of rural England and Europe during the First World War. To coincide with the release of* War Horse, *Shoothill recreated Joey's journey within a unique TimeMap experience for MSN USA.*

## The agency

### Shoothill

Shoothill are experts in developing web-based Microsoft software applications for a wide range of clients. We specialize in data visualization and custom software creation using platforms like Bing Maps and Microsoft Deep Zoom. Many of our products have been world firsts, and we thrive on pushing the boundaries of Microsoft software to create exciting and innovative solutions.

## The project

### The War Horse Journey

The project was titled "The War Horse Journey" and was a joint partnership between Disney (DreamWorks Pictures), MSN USA, 4D (creative) and Shoothill. *War Horse* is a 2011 First World War epic motion picture directed by Steven Spielberg. It is based on both *War Horse*, a children's novel set before and during World War I, by British author Michael Morpurgo, first published in the United

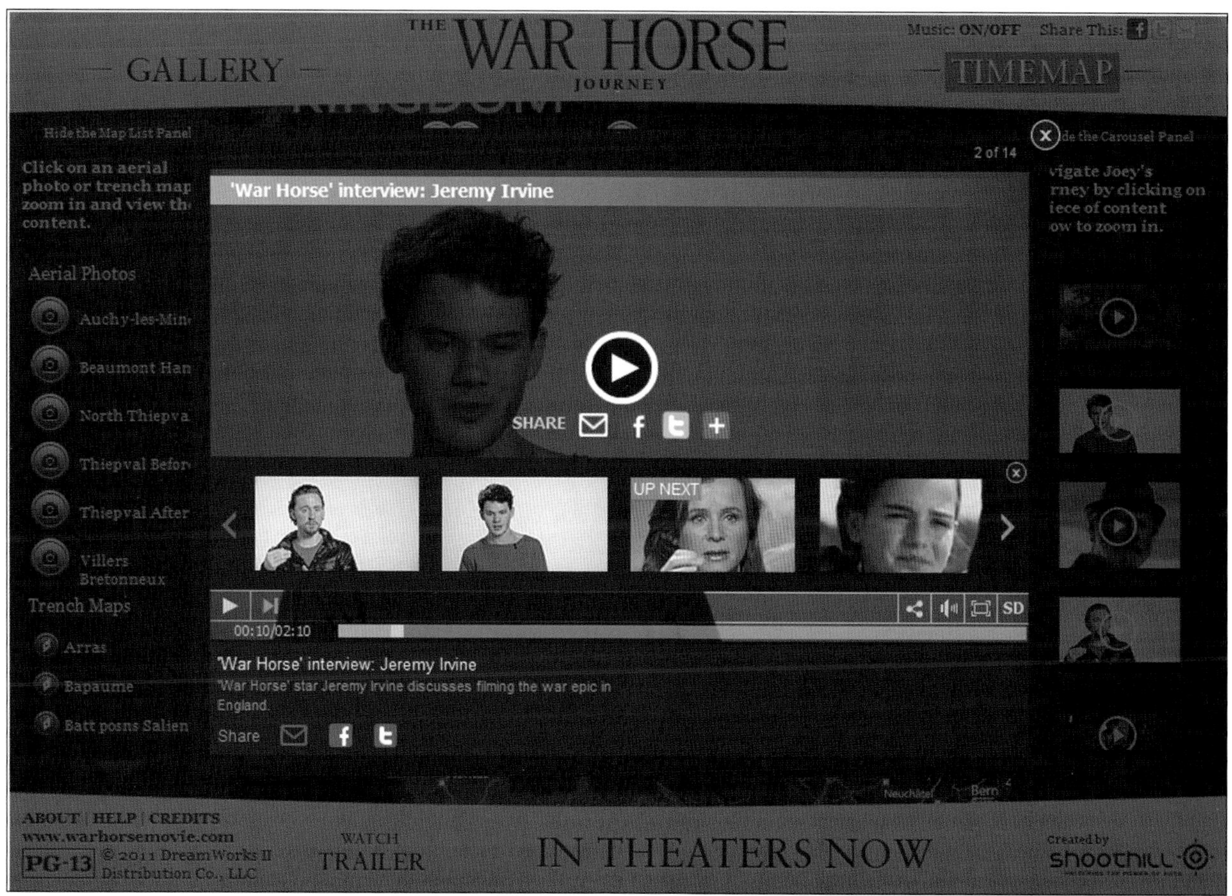


Kingdom in 1982, and the 2007 stage adaptation of the same name.

Disney (DreamWorks Pictures) and their agency, 4D, approached MSN USA to create an online and interactive promotion to coincide with the release of the film in December 2011.

Shoothill, through a close relationship with MSN, was able to pitch several ideas using the latest Microsoft technology, and then we produced some creative storyboards for MSN USA to take to Disney and 4D. Based on these proposals, Disney was delighted with the concept and awarded MSN the contract to promote the movie. Shoothill was engaged to create and deliver the project to MSN, who promoted it across their site.

Disney provided all movie-based assets, including exclusive pictures from the making of the film, video from the movie trailers and interviews with the cast of the film, sketches and storyboards from the pre-production.

MSN provided all landing pages and additional activities (including MSN

page takeovers, Facebook integration and specific War Horse pages on the portal).

Shoothill was responsible for conducting all research and gathering all of the historical elements within the experience, including sourcing the trench maps and aligning them with the "real world" to pinpoint their exact location on Bing maps. This was a difficult task, as many of the maps were slightly inaccurate; some were actually drawn while under fire at the front and many were of poor quality due to their age.

Shoothill also sourced other material, such as the pictures of war horses and aerial photography, as well as the pages from the diaries of cavalry men in the First World War (for these we approached the National Archives in Kew and the Imperial War Museum). Once we had all the content, we then had to edit and process all the images and extracts, researching and writing the captions tailored for each item. Finally, Shoothill then had to place each image into the Deep Zoom gallery.

> **“ The brief was to ‘bring alive’ the story of Joey the horse and his journey from his farm in Devon into the maelstrom of France during the battles of the First World War.**

## The brief

The brief was to “bring alive” the story of Joey the horse and his journey from his farm in Devon into the maelstrom of France during the battles of the First World War.

The client wanted an experience that projected the principles of the friendship between Albert and Joey and the bravery needed to overcome the obstacles they faced. They also wanted something that had never been seen before that would bring home the story of the movie but also add an element of realism and history.

## *How did you interpret the brief?*

MSN USA approached Shoothill to seek our digital creative ideas to pitch for Disney’s upcoming movie *War Horse*—about a boy who is on a mission to find his horse in Europe during WWI. Shoothill came up with the idea of creating a “TimeMap” of the UK, France and Belgium, showcasing maps and aerial imagery from WWI where at certain points on the map the end user would be able to see content from the movie and also historical content from the First World War.

As there was a lot of potential content to display, Shoothill also came up with the idea of a Deep Zoom content wall that would allow users to examine all of the content pieces. Following on from this, all parties agreed that we could incorporate a Deep Zoom Gallery into the experience.

We also went to the National Archives to see what mapping data we could find. Along with the thousands of maps created during the battles, we also found archives

> **“ Rather than focusing on the tragedy of the war and the losses, we were asked to look at the relationships between the men and the horses, the trust and the bravery of both.**

of dairies written by British cavalry officers, which were not only highly interesting but also poignant, as many of the entries in the diaries referred to the incredibly close relationship between the soldiers and their horses, and went so well with the subject material, and both MSN and Disney agreed.

From this, we had additional feedback on how the theme of the experience should be portrayed. Rather than focusing on the tragedy of the war and the losses, we were asked to look at the relationships between the men and the horses, the trust and the bravery of both. In essence, the purpose of The War Horse Journey was to bring history to life.

### *What was your working relationship like with the client?*

Once the project had been confirmed, we worked backwards from the delivery date and created "sprints" for each stage in the development. Once this had been reviewed by all parties, work began, and then at the end of each sprint, we would give a link to the client to see the project and its development at that stage. After these sprints, the client gave regular feedback during conference calls and online meetings, and any change requests were added into the next sprint once the changes had been discussed.

As well as dealing with the third party, we were also able to deal directly with the client, which was fantastic for getting the experience perfect, as they were able to provide us with exclusive content, such as the video clips, images and even the music score from the movie to accompany the experience.

## *For this project did designers deal directly with the client or work through account and project managers?*

For War Horse, the primary contact with the client was through a project manager who was responsible for interpreting the client's wishes to the software developers and graphic designers.

## *During the initial phase of development and try outs for the project, what worked and what didn't?*

Initially, the experience was to be built on the Microsoft Silverlight platform. However, Disney requested that The War Horse Journey should also work on iPads. Unfortunately, iPad does not support Microsoft Silverlight (or Flash), so it was realized that to satisfy this request from the

client, Shoothill would have to build the entire experience using Ajax. As this kind of experience had not been built in Ajax before, to some extent Shoothill was on new ground in attempting to build everything this way. Nonetheless, once it was built and tested, The War Horse Journey ran as well as on the Silverlight platform, so all parties involved were happy with the outcome.

Due to time and distance constraints (i.e., UK and West Coast USA), we mainly used weekly conference calls and online meetings. Although there was a time difference between us and the clients, it worked in our favor (although there were several late nights).

The reason for this is that overnight, to the U.S. teams, we were able to get them updates by the start of the next day, which was fantastic for them as they did not experience any delay when feedback needed to be implemented.

## What was the initial reaction to the project?

The initial reaction to the project was great! Shoothill received some fantastic mentions throughout the social networks and online media. Even after nearly two months of being live, we were still being featured in national media and press.

Roger Ebert (http://en.wikipedia.org/wiki/Roger_Ebert) a Pulitzer Prize-winning and distinguished film critic from the States with 573,476 followers on Twitter, tweeted, "Rather astonishing. A 'War Horse' interactive Time Map."

Due to the fantastic feedback we received, MSN USA decided to host the experience until the DVD release and they plan to promote the experience once again.

# Creative Survival

# *Multidisciplinary working*

> **“I spent the majority of my career as a specialist (art director). This put me at a huge disadvantage once I stepped out of the agency world. I couldn’t produce much of anything without the help of other specialists. My goal for the last year has been to round out my skill set.**
>
> –Brian Hurewitz

## “What would you like to be when you grow up?”

WHEN YOU WERE ASKED that question as a child, chances are you’d have said an astronaut or racing car driver or maybe a ballet dancer or a guitar player. Your young mind would have thought of a very clear singular and quite specialist route for a career, and later your educational route may also have encouraged that focus. The idea of being a jack-of-all-trades would have seemed very much like being a dabbling amateur.

Change is the name of the game in the digital world. Skill sets constantly need refreshing, and the platforms work is seen on by users changes at an astonishing rate.

Keeping up with all the tech advances is a job in itself. This is certainly the wrong industry to be in if you can't embrace change both in and around you. The key to success is to understand that you need to be flexible and become a specialist generalist—in other words, a specialist who can diversify. Painting yourself into a corner by sticking with one niche, specialist skill is a dangerous choice when it comes to future-proofing your career. Core skills combined with a more generalist approach to digital make you a much more attractive proposition to an employer. It makes sense for an agency to want to put together a team of individuals with core competencies who can branch out rather than a team of one-trick ponies who work in a siloed fashion. This "silo" or "pipeline" way of working is where one individual does their specialist bit and then passes it onto another who in turn passes it onto somewhere else. It's a specialist creative conveyor and one that misses out on two essential ingredients for creative working: collaboration and understanding.

If you're a designer working on an interface layout, then having a working knowledge of how it needs to be built and fluidly designed to work on different devices and platforms will save time when it goes into development. You'll also be able to work collaboratively with the developer, as you'll understand his concerns and he'll be able to see where you're trying to get to with the layout. Okay, this might sound a little bit idealized for the real world, but at least you'll both have enough knowledge of what the other does in order to create a level playing field so you can thrash out a solution together.

The convergence of relatable skills between these two areas—design and development—is evident in the new breed of creative technologists, where developers and creative come together. It's a perfect pairing when you come to think of it, as coding is as creative a pursuit as pixel pushing but is rarely thought of as such because it's notoriously hard to show a client that a coder has been creative with code. It's much easier to engage them with a well-designed interface that they can see and mutter over.

It's important for creatives not to see creativity and technology as two separate things. Programmers, coders and creatives need to come together at the initial project kickoff meeting and ask, "What can we do together?" At this point, it becomes truly creative and unrestricted by the knowledge of just one person.

Not so very long ago, designers could produce a Photoshop design and throw it over to a developer who would then be tasked to make all the "magic buttons" work. And more often than not, it would be bounced back to the designer because the function or a tech spec hadn't been figured out before the design was completed. These days because of budget and time restrictions, the creative tech needs to be figured out right from the get-go. This is where the new wave of creative technologists are coming from, which is pretty much a fancy term (and probably a cooler one) than a specialist-generalist.

> **“…I do think in this day and age the visual package a client needs can cross all of these disciplines, so I do think in some cases you do need an all-round vision to service all the client’s needs.**
>
> — Jeff Knowles

What we shouldn’t forget is that dipping your toes into different media and skill sets is also fun. Yes, fun. It’s not a dirty word. If you’re not of the opinion that your creative education ceased when you left university, then learning new stuff can be the best part of the job, as Ross Fordham will tell you:

> *I’d park myself in the generalist category. Opportunities to work in film, digital, sound and space (3-D, not intergalactic) keep the job fresh and challenging. I think developing an individual approach is important, preferably rooted in great ideas, but our world is continually in flux; I wouldn’t want to cut myself off from this.*

Freelancer Franz Jeitz realized he needed a varied bag of skills to break into designing for the music industry:

> *It became clear that you need a lot of different skills to keep getting work. I often get approached to do websites for bands. This isn’t necessarily my favorite aspect of design, but it means that I got a foot in the door and will be considered when it comes to cover designs and gig posters. There are obviously pros and cons for both specialists and generalists. I myself am happy to work on many different projects and learn new skills along the way.*

## It’s not all about software skills

Great ideas still reign supreme over software qualifications. The life of a creative,

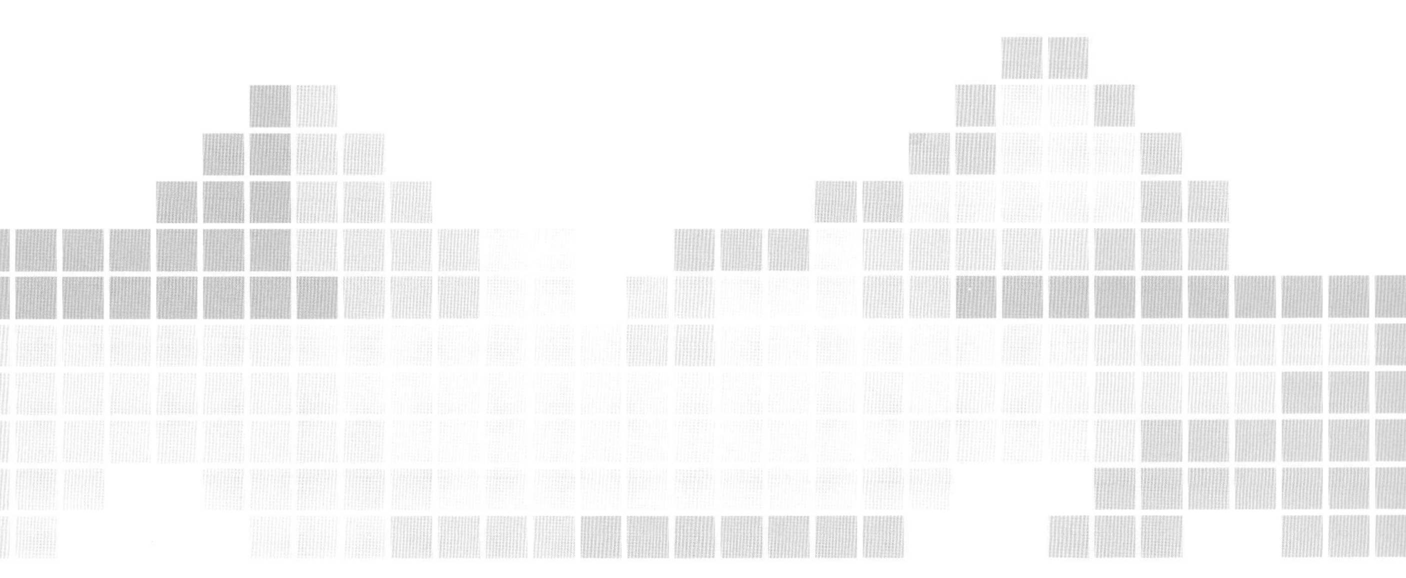

however, doesn't solely depend on their technical bag of tricks. Good ideas are timeless. What has changed is how these are deployed and how your audience interacts with them. A good idea should be the starting point for any creative work. Being a specialist-generalist goes beyond just knowing software. Says Jeff Knowles:

> *I think technically it is very hard to become an all-rounder and have knowledge in print, web, 3-D animation, illustration, etc. You would spend your whole time learning applications. But I do think in this day and age the visual package a client needs can cross all of these disciplines, so I do think in some cases you do need an all-round vision to service all the client's needs.*

Jeff's point is very valid. No sooner would you learn one software package back to front and left to right then it would probably be time for that bit of software to be updated! With software, the trick is to create cheat sheets for the industry standard suite of tools.

Who are these people who know what every drop-down and button does in every bit of software? You certainly don't see them out in the day. Most of us prefer to have an idea and then approach the technology and figure out a way to actualize that idea by using it rather than looking at the technology and seeing what it can do and then bolting a creative idea onto that. Doing the latter makes your work faddish and laden with the out-of-the-box effects,

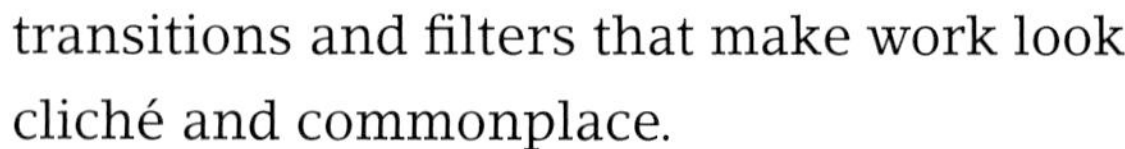

transitions and filters that make work look cliché and commonplace.

If you're pressing that preset filter button, you can bet dollars to doughnuts that many more pixel creatives are doing exactly the same thing. Let's look at it this way: Learning what every button, drop-down and contextual menu in Microsoft Word does won't make you a great author, just as knowing everything about Photoshop won't make you a great artist. You bring the idea to the software and bend and twist the technology to make it happen. (Only try this with software, not with a developer or programmer, as it's very possibly illegal and just not nice.) Figuring out how to do something is much more productive than sitting down with a 500-page software manual. Only a dummy would do that.

## Relatable skills

Being a specialist-generalist in the digital creative world is about having an understanding and working knowledge of key areas that relate to your core skills. If you're a designer of interfaces, then

> **Personally, I think that if you're good at your craft, then you will be able to implement it across different sectors. The lessons learned from working in one area can be invaluable when transferred to another. It opens you up to different ideas and ways of working and helps to stop you becoming complacent and a bit stale. Some clients understand this bigger picture, while others prefer the comfort zone of someone who remains within the boundaries of one sector.**
>
> –Janet Awe

knowing how a user interacts by touch compared to a pointing device and what that means to your design is a relatable skill. If you're a motion graphics designer, it would make sense to understand how your animations could also be formatted to be seen on television rather than just the web, should the need arise to port them across from one medium to another. Ben Curzon explains how this applies in the creative and advertising industry today:

*It's certainly vital to have a broad understanding of all touch points, but as a vocation, you still need to have clear focus on one path. For example, a good UX designer needs to understand all aspects of a project from interaction, business strategy, marketing, visual design, development and technology, but ultimately their core role is to ensure the end user receives the best experience possible by aligning all of these things as well and suitably as can be achieved. They don't need to be fluent in HTML or .net because there are others working as part of the project that will be. Know what everyone involved does and use and manage their skills accordingly.*

You also need to understand every medium that can be used to get your message across. The learning curve is continual, but as Miranda Bolter points out:

*Far from seeing this as a pressure, I think it's hugely productive. I never want to feel that I've stopped learning. I think I'd get bored.*

## Cogs in the machine & the bigger picture

Driving innovation is usually the domain of the generalist, as they have a clearer view of the bigger creative picture. The best creative leaders will be generalists (or perhaps "generals" to use the similarly bestowed military title) as they can coordinate and appreciate how all the cogs of the creative wheel come together. A creative leader may not be the best illustrator but they will understand what software is used to create the artwork, how long a piece of work should take and what the challenges of that work are. If they were pushed and their team were all suddenly sent home ill with some creative malaise, they could theoretically step in and be both head cook and chief bottle washer and make sure the cogs kept on turning. With a team of specialist-generalists, a certain amount of flexibility is afforded to the agency when it comes to delivery of work. When it comes to idea generation, those with a greater breadth of experience will think in much broader strokes than their specialist colleagues.

## Learning on the job

Education doesn't end on the last day of

university or college. It's only the start. There are so many learning opportunities in the creative industry, you'll find that even if you've completely specialized at university you'll be acquiring new skills as soon as you become involved in projects. You could go from being somebody who was graphics oriented to becoming involved in conceptualizing, storyboarding and animating. As soon as you start collaborating, you begin to understand what another creative does and the processes they follow. If you're savvy, you'll also ask lots of questions—not too many to be annoying but enough to learn how your fellow creative works. This is where flexibility is so important. Sticking your hand up and saying, "Hey, I'm the graphics guy. I do graphics and that's that" won't earn you any favors, as Caroline Annis notes:

*If you have a good reputation and people want to use you again, then they prioritize this over the fact that you don't have the specialist skills for a particular job. Most people, clients and agencies, would rather work with someone who is trusted than someone who has one set of unique skills. This gives you a wider experience, which is no bad thing. It is possible to become more generalist without losing your creative edge.*

When asked which one essential skill is needed to work in digital creative, Natalie Jahangiry replies:

*A smile, even in the most stressful times…*

Even though that might be well and truly a forced smile at times, it will in fact diffuse

> **I personally feel learning more within my field—for example programming—not only broadens my skills and makes me more marketable, it also makes me look at things from a different angle....it's important to always be learning, regardless of specialism.**
>
> — Ben Powell

many a situation. Combine it with a "can do" generalist approach and you won't end up painting yourself in a corner with your skill set. You'll also be more likely to be given the better and more challenging projects. You wouldn't want to be known as the guy that only makes animated banners, would you? Someone who makes them all day ... every day ... You may as well get a job in a factory making can openers, as it would have pretty much the same creative challenges to it.

Working in creative isn't like being an accountant or a butcher. You don't stop doing it when you go home. It's a career that's a little obsessive. It's with you all the time as you make connections between shape and form and ideas. Everything can inspire you, and that creative restlessness will encourage you to want to learn to make things out of digital nothingness. It's the absolute joy of the job that at the start of the day there's a blank page and by day's end there's an idea on the page in words, code or visuals.

You'll naturally become more of an all-rounder the longer you work in the industry, which in turn makes you and your creative talents more marketable.

## A flexible approach

Digital agencies need to be flexible. With staff and mounting overheads, it makes

## *JOSEPH R. LUCK : SOUNDING OUT THE WEB*

**Biography:** *Joe is currently a full-time student studying sound design at Ravensbourne College of Design and Communication. Joe believes that having a degree isn't enough to guarantee work in a creative industry and that experience is equally, if not more, desirable. He also specializes in web design and development. In conjunction with university study, he provides a range of audio and web services through Joseph Luck Design. His clients include the RSA, Future Publishing, Made by Many, Knight Studios, Awake-London and Enigmati Inc. Outside of audio, Joe has a portfolio primarily of personal and small business websites. www.josephluck.co.uk*

As a student at a creative outlet, being multidisciplined is highly encouraged, so yes I do feel the pressure but I think that it's equally important to have a primary skill set. While studying for a degree, I use my free time to find real work and contracts. For example, I landed a lengthy contract with Enigmati Inc, designing sound effects for their iOS and Android game. I had no formal training in audio implementation, audio programming or game engines prior to this, but my computing background allowed me to adapt and learn these new skills on the job, and I will be able to apply these in the future.

It's important for me, at the foundations of my career, to be able to say yes to work, primarily to network. In order to stay ahead of the competition in my disciplines, it's also vital to find a comfortable balance between being a generalist or a specialist. This is why I think it's more difficult to be a professional in multiple disciplines without already being regarded as an expert in a single field.

I think that people are starting to believe that "having their fingers in many pies" will one day land them a high-profile job, which will secure future work in that industry. I think it's a result of harsh competition from large amounts of people wanting to do the same thing. With companies and agencies, it's all about budget, and what I mean by that is a production company will be more likely to hire someone who knows how to use a camera in conjunction with a solid knowledge of audio than someone who just possesses the audio prowess.

sense for them to look at recruiting specialist-generalists. If Sarah worked purely on web graphics and is off sick for three days, then the whole project stalls. If Luke, who specializes in animation, can also create web graphics, then he can easily take over, and money and time won't be lost. On the big accountancy balance sheet, this makes sense for any agency. Ben Powell notes that:

> *I personally feel learning more within my field—for example programming—not only broadens my skills and makes me more marketable, it also makes me look at things from a different angle, which is beneficial both in my work as a freelancer and for a company; it's important to always be learning, regardless of specialism.*

It's a competitive industry and when combined with a tough economic climate, it can be dangerous to stand still and not be flexible with your skill set as a digital creative. An agency that has a team of multidisciplined creative workers becomes an attractive proposition to a client if they can deliver a complete brand solution. If the brief includes an app, video content, web and perhaps a mobile offering, the agency or freelancer who can turn their hand to the various demands of the brief and become almost a "one-stop shop" for the client becomes empowered by offering a complete solution. It's a time and money saver in many respects, both for the client and the agency or freelancer, as asset management becomes easier. The creative cycle of a project remains under one roof without having to involve another agency or specialist. It's a time saver as the project can

## *NATALIE JAHANGIRY: DIVERSIFYING SKILLS*

**Biography:** *Natalie graduated from Northumbria University in multimedia design in 2008 and became a London-based designer shortly after this. Her time in the industry so far has seen her delivering successful design communication solutions for well-known organizations such as Virgin Media, BBC, Disney, NSPCC, Burger King, UNICEF, Bacardi, Cadbury and Sky. Natalie currently works for a large global agency based in West London on a range of media from print and DM to social, mobile and web. www.nataliejahangiry.com*

Having a range of skills both conceptual and technical keeps you interested as a designer. It allows you to pick up the cool projects that come in, no matter what category they fall into, and you have such a varied working week. It's important, as it makes for a better portfolio of projects for more than one client and stops you from being shoehorned into one aspect of design.

I have been lucky in the companies I have worked for, as they have allowed me to work with clients who often want a campaign that stretches over all media, and to be involved in this from beginning to end, over all design aspects, gives you a greater sense of satisfaction rather than doing one area and passing it on to the next designer to finish what you created. The first campaign I worked on in my first agency was for Cadbury, where I worked (obviously with help) from the ideas stage, to storyboarding, to creating a look and feel, to website design, to working with a 3-D designer, to creating print pieces/various small print elements to launching the campaign. Getting involved at the start of the project gave me a greater understanding of the idea and how to design this from the start.

Since then, my industry work and personal portfolio consists of a range of skills in different aspects of design: storyboarding and idea generation for companies such as BBC and Barclaycard; web design and pitch work (for example creating a website pitch piece for UNICEF for a Christmas campaign, a campaign website for the new incentive from Virgin called Virgin Tickles and an e-commerce site for my brother's clothing line FAWN Couture); mobile design for Bacardi Oakheart and a Burger King iPhone app; print advertising in-store for Phillips, direct mail packs for NSPCC and Guide Dogs and sales brochures for my family's property company Hits International; social media sites on Facebook for Bacardi at festivals and an Iron Man competition for Burger King; promotional e-mail design for Sky, Petplan and Disney; campaign branding for Barclaycard and many more.

> **I need to be an all-rounder as a PM, and this suits my personality, as I love being involved in a variety of different things and there are always new things to learn if you're flexible.**
>
> — Sam Peliza

be managed by the same project manager (PM), and the process of handing over assets from one creative to another isn't held up by waiting for someone else in another agency to finish their part of the job. For PMs, it's essential to become a shape shifter and be able to adapt and be flexible. Sam Peliza knows this from experience:

> *I need to be an all-rounder as a PM, and this suits my personality, as I love being involved in a variety of different things and there are always new things to learn if you're flexible. I have to work with all types of personalities and have an understanding of lots of different skills.*

## An understanding of job specs

Look at any advert for a "digital designer" or "digital creative" and alongside the core skills required for that job you'll be dazzled by the shopping list of "desirable skills" or "nice to haves" that stretch out below it. Some are veritable wish lists. You can almost see and hear the meeting that took place to write that ad: "Okay, yeah Mark, can you ask Pete in accounts what he thinks? Do they need to know Facebook network interoperability and what about thermo nuclear fusion? Oh and don't forget they need to tote that barge and lift that bale."

It's the equivalent of putting an ad in for a nanny and asking for Mary Poppins.

It's generalist skills gone mad, and the problem with this is usually they're not relatable skills to the job advertised in the first place. It's fine for a recruitment

## *RACHEL SHILLCOCK: KNOWING WHAT TO KNOW AND WHAT NOT TO*

**Biography:** *Rachel Shillcock is a designer and front-end developer from Manchester, UK. She is a published logo designer and writer, appearing in books and magazines such as* Logo Design Volume 3 *and* .net *magazine. Rachel has worked as a web designer and front-end developer for agencies in Manchester, including an SEO agency and full-service agency, as well as freelancing for local and online businesses and personalities. In her spare time, Rachel is a photography enthusiast who enjoys taking long walks around the countryside with her camera and tripod in hand. Visit her online blog and website at www.rachil.li.*

Overall having the ability to flick between different areas of design gives you variation, keeps you fresh and allows you to have a greater understanding of the projects and clients as a whole.

I think there is so much conflicting advice on whether you should specialize in specific subjects or have a wide variety of skills that it's impossible to give a definitive answer about this anymore. I think that there are subtle pressures at play, and this is through simple things such as job adverts and job titles. A few years ago, job titles were a simple way of determining somebody's skill set. A web designer, for example, would design websites. Nowadays, this is much more ambiguous and difficult to figure out. A web designer now might wireframe, design, build prototypes or fully working websites in HTML and CSS and even know JavaScript libraries such as jQuery. You could say that this is simply because expectations have risen, but I think that it's a combination of how much the web has grown and how we have to adapt and grow to keep up with the demand of what is now possible on the web. It's no longer good enough to be good at one thing—the competition out there is so strong that we need to make sure we excel at what we can do, and sometimes this may involve learning new skills and technologies.

A few years ago I fell into the trap of thinking that I had to fit into as many skill sets as possible. This meant that if you'd asked me what I "did," I would tell you that I worked on graphic design, web design, web development, and animation and motion graphics. The problem with this is that you start to define yourself as a "jack-of-all-trades and master of none." Now I understand the importance of working to your strengths; I know that I would explain to people how I work on what I am good at—design (web and graphic) and front-end development.

consultant to want to get some bang for their buck with a candidate, but it's important to clarify to what extent these "nice to haves" need to be known before going to an interview. Johnny Issacs knows the problem only too well:

> *You only have to look at what agencies and studios want from juniors these days to see the trend and, in my opinion, the problem. I have seen studios asking for juniors to know the Creative Suite, HTML & CSS, JavaScript and jQuery, 3-D modeling (if possible) and on top of that to have at least two years' experience. With requirements like that on many if not most of the jobs that I have seen advertised, I would say that there is an immense pressure to be an all-rounder. The problem is that you cannot do it all.*

The interactive designer job spec is certainly not a standard one across the industry; when it comes to asking for an "understanding of" other nonrelatable skills it can become highly contentious. Most of us can understand the third law of thermodynamics if it's explained using simple words and puppets, but we wouldn't necessarily then want to explain it to anybody else in detail. When going for a job, it's important to explain what your core skills are to prove you're adaptable but also to ask to what degree the "nice to haves" need to be known and how they relate to the job at hand. Why is 3-D modeling even on the list of "nice to haves" skills for a junior position? It's not relatable. They may as well be asked to have goat herding skills, as it also isn't an extendable skill from being a junior digital creative. It's like asking a butcher to be a baker and the baker to be a candlestick maker.

You also don't want to get the job on the strength of your core skills and then on arrival spend most of your time doing specialist work in your secondary skills area. I got suckered into this trap completely at a top-ten agency in London. Hired to be a senior art director, my comment in the interview that I knew Flash and could animate (indeed I do) resulted in me spending eight months churning out animated banner ads. They were actually looking for a Flash designer but thought they needed a senior art director—then they thought they could have both but realized they only wanted a banner maker. It was a particularly messed up recruitment brief, which I ended up suffering because of.

Sometimes recruitment briefs (especially client-side I have to say) are put together by committee. That's rather a grand-sounding statement, for what it actually means is that an e-mail goes round the office or senior management asking, "What shall we ask for?" I remember receiving an e-mail like this once, where one senior figure on an ad for an animator put "They need to know how fix e-mail," which I hear is the leading skill required to work at Pixar.

You have to go into an interview and not be afraid to ask what exactly they're looking for; be flexible and open to adapting your skill set, but make sure what they're asking for is actually what you'll be doing and what they want.

## Three routes to success

*Usually when pitching for a creative job, the brief comes in and an agency will respond by producing three creative routes that explore it. All these routes match the brief but push the work in different directions. Generally the three routes will be given to separate designers to develop and are something like this:*

### Route One: "Let's play it safe"

This safe route, which ticks all the boxes of the brief but probably isn't very progressive, will do the job quickly, efficiently and to budget. As a designer, this is probably the most boring route to have to work on.

### Route Two: "Blue sky ideas"

This route clings to the brief by the skin of its teeth but brings in new technologies, left-field thinking and radical ideas, which push, and in most cases improve, the brief beyond its current state. This is the cool route to work on. Provided you stick to the mandatory goals of the brief, you can push and shape it as you see fit. Throw all the ideas in there from your creative box of tricks and make something that has a "wow" factor to it.

## Route Three: "Safe but with a bit of an edge"

This route is usually a hybrid of routes one and two. You want to give the client a dollop of "safe" with a smattering of "slightly edgy" ( a term loved by clients, which essentially means "make it a little daring… but don't go too far"). More useless buzzwords you might hear are "pop," "standout" and "immersive." Pretty much they all mean "Make it safe but not that safe; oh, and make people like it."

"Why bother with three routes?" you might be asking. Well, when responding to a brief, it's good to show that you understand its goals and the deliverables (Route 1) and that you also are an agency/freelancer who has big ideas and can make a client go "wow" with the breadth of knowledge of technology and creative (Route 2) but you also know how to ground those ideas and make them workable (Route 3).

### Stratospheric ideas

Blue sky ideas never usually fully see the light of day, but you'll find that clients enjoy the fact that you're flexing your creative muscle, and this can act as a convincer for them to go with the slightly tamer third route. Knowing that you can have those big ideas will encourage the client to want to work with you again. You are an amazing creative, after all. Just make sure that however blue sky the idea, it covers what's asked for in the current brief or rationalizes why it doesn't just so that doesn't become a sticking point when it comes to feedback. It can then leap off into diverse directions and

**More often than not, [the blue sky idea] will need to be pared down a little from the original pitch, as a lot of designers will subscribe to the notion that the big idea should push the technology rather than being held back by it.**

become something much better than the original client brief.

Of course, once in a while, there is that rare, delightful client who will want to go with the blue sky thinking route. More often than not, this will need to be pared down a little from the original pitch, as a lot of designers will subscribe to the notion that the big idea should push the technology rather than being held back by it. This is a marvelous ideal, but it can go fantastically wrong if you don't at least run your idea past a developer to see if it's doable with the technology we currently have in the twenty-first century.

I was tasked once with putting together the blue sky route for a pitch while working on a music website. I wanted to use an animation on the home page that would deliver rotational news stories. I didn't want the same old boring element, which just flipped over and wham there was another story. Instead I had the idea of using a sine wave visualization animation that would twist and turn and be reactive to whatever the computer's microphone was picking up. It would then associate certain sound cues to certain news stories. So it would, in effect, be bringing you a news story that had some relation to the sound of your surroundings. Not wanting to sell myself down the river should the idea go through, I did a lot of research on different sound key technologies and how this idea could potentially be made. I also went and spoke to a developer (which is something I would always recommend) who told me it could potentially be developed but it would take work (and a large budget). Having developers looped in even at this point gives them a sense of being involved at the grassroots of a project and eases the discussions later on should the pitch be won and the idea goes into development.

My blue sky route was the one they chose because my presentation included a tech rationale in it. My idea went completely soaring off into space but I hadn't let it go into the realms of "undoable."

One incident where the lack of any technical knowledge became spectacularly embarrassing for the designer involved happened when I was working client-side for a dot com boom Internet portal. An agency had come in to present some ideas for a campaign we were working on for a large coffee manufacturer. The ideas bubbled along until they got to their blue sky route. With an elaborate flourish, the designer waved dramatically at us and declared "and with Flash animation technology we will have the web page fill up with the sight, sound and smell of coffee."

"Excuse me … the what?"

"The SMELL."

"I mean ... is that even possible? The smell? Really?!"

The idea was quite frankly off its rocker and sadly negated everything else they'd shown us previously. Talking to a developer is a good idea especially if you want to avoid claims of advances in smell-o-vision technology.

It's important to keep up generally with technology, apps, web trends and who is doing what in the industry, as you need to be fully versed and passionate about this. This business is becoming more and more multidisciplinary, so a 360-degree take on the business will be a lifeline should you find yourself having to redevelop your skill set and change your own personal "offering" to an employer. Keep your head over the parapet when it comes to watching the changes and turns that happen in the industry. Roll with the punches; don't try to fight against them.

## Three routes, one designer

The routes mentioned above have clear lines of division, but it's not always the case that they're so defined. A designer could be given a job where they have to create three routes themselves. This puts terrible pressure on anyone assigned to do this because it's a lot of work to think through three routes fully in a short period of time. At least one of the routes will be rushed, as it's usually the case that a designer will prefer one of their routes more than another and will shower it with time and energy and rush the also-ran one.

In this instance, try and push back with your creative director and use the rationale that it's best to free up resources to tackle the brief by three people rather than just one, as the routes will be better realized rather than being rushed by one person, which could put the eventual pitch in danger.

## Rationale

A rationale is a summation, usually written by the designer, of their proposed idea or route for a pitch. It's important for a number of good reasons—particularly when the designer in question isn't presenting the work to the client or the presentation is being e-mailed to a client.

If you balk at the idea of writing, you can make this a little easier on yourself by following this outline:

Give the route a name if it doesn't already have one. If you've been working on the safe route, DON'T call it that when it goes client-side. Look at the styles you've used or at a key part of the project's functionality and have the name reflect something to do with that.

You need an opening preamble to set the tone, but try and keep it short. Explain what inspired you to create your design or devise the functionality used. Keep it in plain English and don't waffle on with language that is overly prosaic. You don't want your rationale to put the client off your work.

Explain how this meets, enhances or exceeds the end user's needs. So if it's a website where you can design your own T-shirt, explain how the mechanics of setting up and ordering a T-shirt has been simplified into three clicks, so the site visitor can spend more time being creative designing their T-shirt rather than fussing around with the ordering process.

Do the tech. Add a line or two here about how the technology driving your route works. Don't make any big claims or promises (remember the coffee story); remember this could come back to bite you on the backside.

Wrap up your rationale with a line that is the equivalent of "Pick me because..." but not as overt. Sum up what your route offers and its key benefits.

In your rationale, don't cast doubts on your own work or add route-killing lines such as "This will obviously look much better when it's fully artworked up and if we had more time." No. No and No. Have a colleague proofread the rationale for you and then ask them questions about it, such as "What are the project goals and how have I met them?," "How does my route work technically?" and "What was the inspiration behind this route?" You're covered if they can answer these questions.

## You don't need to tell me that

Some work quite literally speaks for itself. Rationales become nonsense when applied to work such as online campaign works where you've a set of banners communicating a message. If you have to write a rationale to explain what they're doing, then they're not doing what they should be doing! Overexplaining ideas can make them appear complicated even if they're actually quite straightforward in their execution. It's a pitfall best avoided.

## Pulling a rabbit out of the hat: The art of repurposing

The canny creative knows that all those blue-sky ideas need to be pocketed away for a rainy day when a blue sky would be most welcome. There's been more than one occasion in my career when a keen as mustard project manager goes to lunch with an existing, well-established client and decides to "drop back to the studio with them" and perhaps if there's time could we "show them something." This usually happens around 3 p.m. on a Friday and is the effect of a big meal and white wine bonhomie. At this point, the studio goes into panic. There's no plan, there's no brief but there's been some vague conversation on the phone about this company celebrating a hundred years of business soon and what could we do for them?

This is where you just need some ideas and visuals—fast! What the project manager really wants to do is show the client "pretty things" to keep their interest and show what the team could do.

Repurposing is the art of taking existing ideas or visuals and turning them into placeholders for Mac visuals or worked up scamps for another campaign. Film directors often take soundtracks from other movies and use them as placeholders to help set tone and give the composer who is preparing the score an idea of what they're after for the eventual movie. What you're trying to do here is look through your back catalogue of creative, functionality and ideas to start the ball rolling with the creative discussion. There may be a way of using that existing functionality that was created but never used for such and such a campaign, or perhaps that idea with the clock from a pitch that was never used could work for this campaign?

By keeping all those blue-sky ideas safe, you'll always have creative ideas to start a sudden and unexpected client meeting off with. It's a very quick way to put pretty things in front of a client to start the creative ball rolling, or if you're having to pull together a presentation document full of creative, then use this creative to make it look … pretty.

## Brought to book

A creative sketchbook is a must for any digital creative. Take it to work meetings, when you're on the bus, the train, at home and doodle in it, draw stuff (however rough), write down ideas and make meeting notes in it. It's a brain dump book that can help trigger an idea when you need one fast. If a brief comes in for a two-week campaign and it needs to start in three days, then look through your book and see if there's anything suitable or a half-formed idea that, with a bit of work, would suit the campaign.

## Templates

Most developers keep code libraries. It makes perfect sense to do so, especially since so much is reused in the work they do. It saves having to repeat and write long laborious passages of code over and over again for different projects. Quite frankly it can be a chore to keep setting up files. Digital creatives save a lot of time by keeping hold of Photoshop grid layouts for websites and mobile devices. It's a time saver and lets you get straight to the creative work rather than messing around with a template. You never know when that unused web design you created last spring may come in handy again. Delete nothing!

# Show some client love (and hate)

**AS CREATIVES**, we all, at some point, will moan about clients. We become exasperated that they just don't "get" us or understand creatively our vision or "how good this could be!" This type of pouting isn't unusual but we have to ask ourselves if we're being transparent enough with our work and ideas so they will "get us" or if we've communicated our vision effectively enough using presentations, sketches, scamps and mood boards. Could we perhaps use something else (mime? or how about ... puppets?) to express our ideas and ways of working? If you've tried all that and still they're not up to speed with you, then perhaps the moaning is justified after all ...

## It's their money

You're providing a creative service for somebody else's money. Even if you are going to rewrite the brief at some stage and give your client an amazing piece of work (one that they weren't even aware they needed), the money for that is coming from them. How would you feel if you walked into a bar and ordered a bottle of beer and the barman poured it out without you being able to see what he was doing, drank half of it in front of you and then threw the rest of it in your face and demanded payment? Keep the client in the loop so they know their money is entrusted with the right creative people and they are in fact getting (added) value for money.

## Nuts, whole hazel nuts

There are, of course, clients who are a little bit strange. I remember one who refused to meet unless they could bring a (random) friend along. We would always meet in a restaurant and the friend, apart from ordering their food, would never utter a word. We'd spend an excruciating hour eating in awkward silence before I'd be allowed to talk about the ideas I'd worked up. Afterwards the client would look at his friend then look at me and excuse both of them after which they'd both leave me with only the bill for company. The work however was creatively stimulating and they always paid on time so apart from these "quirks," the client/creative relationship was a very good one. The lesson here is that the behavior I found so out of the ordinary was completely ordinary to them. So challenge your own preconceptions of what people should be like, unless of course they're frothing at the mouth and keep calling you "Mom." This would be a sign that it's time to leave.

## Sign this

An agency would never take on a job without a contract and a statement of work signed by them and the client. If you're freelancing, you may well have experienced the problems of jobs being canceled, clients not paying or a project that should take three weeks actually taking nine. As a freelancer, protect yourself with something on paper with the client's signature on it. I've made the mistake of producing work on trust for a long-term client who would "send a purchase order next week," only never to do so and then to refuse payment. It's a horrible state of affairs to have a long-term relationship severed by a situation such as this, so whoever they are and regardless of how long you've worked with them, have a job contract drawn up or at the very least something on paper that is signed.

## The ace up your sleeve

Box clever and undersell and overdeliver. Give the client enough creative goodness

**This is the added value that makes you look even more like a creative genius and ensures you "overdeliver" on the creative brief.**

and brilliance to sell them your idea but keep part of the idea under wraps.

This ace up your sleeve (perhaps it's a new type of functionality, a unique way of displaying type or a lateral bit of thinking to a rather mundane problem) can be revealed once you're doing the job.

This is the added value that makes you look even more like a creative genius and ensures you "overdeliver" on the creative brief.

## You're fired

Just like any relationship, it's all about give and take. Perhaps the client's right and maybe the logo does need to be bigger? After all, they did listen to you when you said their current website was rubbish. But if it's getting a little bit one-sided and you're continually pestered at the weekend, during the evening, when you're in the shower or walking the dog, then perhaps for your own quality of life it's time to part company. If

you managed to secure that client in the first place, chances are you're talented and articulate enough to secure another one. End the relationship cleanly and professionally, and in a very straightforward way, explain why it's ending. Don't become emotional or confrontational about it and certainly don't meet them in their office boardroom, climb on the table and urinate on their potted palms as once happened in a very large ad agency in London. That would be an example of a very bad way to end a client relationship.

## Is that considered feedback?

### Don't flap

If you're presenting informally at your desk to your creative director and an account manager, try to control your nerves as these can actively work against you receiving good feedback. Don't let your hands flap all over the work. This is a form of diversion and distraction and is almost sleight of hand in its execution.

Subconsciously you're trying to divert attention away from the work. If you need to point, do it to draw the critiquing eyeballs to a part of the work you want to highlight. Be clear and decisive as to which detailed parts of the work or its functionality you're showing.

### Don't tell them what they could have had

How awful would Christmas day be if you were told about all the presents you could have had. "Here's a pair of socks but I was thinking of buying you a Ferrari but I thought I'd go with these instead." Similarly, when presenting ideas routes internally for a brief, don't bombard your audience with a hundred tons of other routes you could have explored. Stick to the ones you've chosen and show confidence in these.

### … And this is a magic button

Magic buttons are the equivalent of the Monopoly board's "Get out of jail free" cards.

They're mostly stuck into a wireframe as an afterthought during an initial presentation when some fatal bit of functionality has been forgotten and this button "will do the trick." If something is glaringly wrong or looks bolted on, it'll stand out like a sore thumb and become the focus of the feedback. Even further down the line when the project is more developed, this "issue" of the button (or whatever it is) will come back to haunt you. Consider elements or functionality like this before an internal presentation.

## Taking it personally

The standard advice here proffered by many is not to take criticism of your work personally but instead to approach bad feedback with a zenlike state of divinity. For the Earthbound amongst us, we most certainly will take bad feedback personally. In life whenever we create something—be it knitting a jumper, baking a cake or designing a website—it becomes part of who we are. Before that website design existed, there was just a blank screen. Your thoughts, talent and instincts made something appear out of nothing. Doing this is an ego-driven process, as you invest so much of your heart and soul into producing in pixels what has previously only been in your head. The ego part of things is connected to the passion behind the creativity, so it's very hard to zen out and always take bad feedback on the chin.

## THE WORST TYPES OF CREATIVE FEEDBACK

I remember once having a client meeting where I showed them some initial concepts for a logo design. He said he liked them, but then proceeded to draw three diagonally aligned circles with a line through them and saying, "Now the logo shouldn't look anything like this, but this is the direction we're going in." Still to this day I have no idea what he meant.

**— Ben Powell**

The most indiscernible feedback I've ever received from a creative director was, "Art direct the fucking thing!"

**— Brian Hurewitz**

One creative director at an agency I've worked for had a fearsome reputation for being brutally honest—honest to the point of reducing people to tears. While that's never brought out the best in me, I do appreciate people who speak their minds and let you know exactly how they feel. You can't be too sensitive or precious about your work. It needs to stand up to interrogation. It's much worse to work for someone who can't make a decision or won't say what they really think for fear of being unpopular. It wastes time in the long run and you won't get the best result.

**— Miranda Bolter**

I like the warmth and dance that comes with the subtleties of the British indirect communication methods. Pleasantries are what make us. Speak in poetic code to your clients and frankly with your project manager. Then have them deal with it.

**— Ben Curzon**

Silence is never good. But elaboration on what the silence means can be even worse. For example:

"So, that's obviously the rough, development work. When are you getting started on the final designs?"

"We're gonna have to phone (client's name) and move the meeting back to next week."

**— Leon Bahrani**

One of the things that I hate is when people beat around the bush. If something is shit, tell me it's shit because, trust me, I will afford you the same courtesy. I think that people get too caught up in protecting the feelings of others in the design world. What they forget though is that the work isn't about us a lot of the time. One of the phrases I positively 100 percent loathe is, "There is something about it. You know?" No, I don't know. Articulate what you love about it, what you hate about it, and eventually we will get to the point where we can clearly see why it is that you like it. It drives me barmy when people say they think something is great but cannot give a reason. One word I also don't like to hear when referring to work is, in fact, the word "like." It is so insipid and weak. It is neither one nor the other. I would rather someone told me that it was the most vile and putrid design they had ever seen than tell me that they "like" it.

**— Johnny Issacs**

The opening line, "That's all great, just one little thing..." is akin to the classic "I'm not a racist, but..." You just know it's going to be followed by a stream of changes that will most likely undo all your good work. I'm sure that sometimes clients feel obliged to request changes to work purely for the sake of it. I've seen feedback like, "Can we make the text bigger but bring the font size down?," "Make it look more modern with a classic feel" and "Make the text sharper but less defined." Another classic critique is, "Make it better."

**— Steve Alexander**

One client always concludes a project brief by saying, "Look forward to the results of the magic wand." Hmmmmmmm...!

**— Jeff Knowles**

My favorite was from a client who wanted us to design their website and said how much they liked it, and then we heard the following week from our friends who were developing the site that the client hated our work and had no intention of using it. They paid us ... but never used it. How weird is that? The other great thing that often happens is when you say something in a group meeting, only to hear whoever the top dog in the room is repeat it later as if it was their idea ... It happens waaaay more than it should.

**— Nat Hunter**

An old creative director of mine literally just strung words together, incomprehensible nonsense with the occasional smattering of "more" and "attitude."

**— Ross Fordham**

The most frustrating experience I have with criticism is that it can be so, so vague. Feedback such as "That doesn't look right" or "It needs to be perfect" without any validation, reasoning or explanation is the most difficult feedback to analyze and work with. Generally, other feedback can be reasoned with or compromised on, but I think that being given vague feedback is the killer. It's hard to work with but also means that you could work for hours improving your design, without knowing what feedback you're going to receive again. Try and work around this by answering with questions and—as hard as it will be—trying to interpret what feedback you do receive. Try and read between the lines and pick out the smallest, tiniest details you can and use this to help you improve the designs where possible.

**— Rachel Shillcock**

# "You can't polish a turd with an HD sparkle"

**WE'VE ALL BECOME** a little obsessed with megapixels and high-definition images and video footage. The general misconception is that if it's not in HD, it might as well be second best. What we tend to forget is that a "good" creative shouldn't just rely on their box of electronic magic (software) tricks. A badly composed and framed shot at high definition is just that. A bad image. No CMOS sensor or millions of megapixels will save it. The truth of any image is found in the story it tells us. Shots that amuse, juxtapose, delight and intrigue are timeless, and their "truth" is irrespective of whether it's in HD or not.

## HD: The obsession

Ask any image maker why they want to work with the best kit, the largest image sensors and all the bells and whistles that come with prosumer DSLRs and video cameras and they'll often be found hankering with a need to recreate the beauty of 35mm film. The dreamy fantastical look of celluloid and the highly saturated Technicolor film process is a staple ingredient of popular culture from the 1950s and 1960s. Some jaw-dropping, delightful pure-analogue beauty has been captured on film. But the 35mm film stock, color process, lenses and lighting are all creative tools. No director turned up on set and thought, It's going to look great anyway, as it's on 35mm. They've carefully thought how these tools would be used to tell a story. The depth of field was carefully chosen to pull out an element from the composition and bring it to the foreground—unlike today where the fashion is to blur everything because most DSLRs can do this. Just because they can doesn't mean it has a place in all of your images' making. Think of these tools as aids to your creative expression and use them in moderation and when you absolutely need them. A small, inexpensive point-and-shoot camera still has the power to bag a nicely framed honest shot, as composition is king and everything else is a little bit of gloss on the top.

# Best practices for sketches, wireframing and mood boards

**THE SHOCK OF THE OLD** informing the new is something that can take a while to become used to in any creative studio. Chopping up foam board and using spray mount adhesive to bind images to board might seem like a blast from a bygone time of creativity, but it's an essential skill for most twenty-first-century creatives. The reason for this is that the tactility of producing something such as a sketch or board of images is something unique. Clients like the idea of being able to feel and touch and point at something that has been "made," which adds value to what you're presenting. The shock of the "real" can also add value to any client meeting. We're so used to looking at screens that being given a sketch on paper that we can hold and touch is a welcome change.

Sketches are commonly used in wireframing and storyboarding. It's a free-form way of working and much better than straight off the bat showing a client Mac visuals. It opens up the creative discussion a bit more, and even the client can take a pen and add to the sketch or wireframe to add their ideas into the pot of creativity. If you're producing website mock-ups and aren't very dexterous with a pencil, then head over to www.balsamiq.com. Balsamiq is a powerful website mock-up creator that renders your work as a sketch and can be easily tweaked and changed when you've received client feedback.

## Mood boards

Life would be a lot simpler if we could read each other's minds. Unfortunately, we can't, which means communicating a creative idea that you've visualized in your head requires certain tools of expression to help a client, creative director or colleague get inside your head and share that vision. Mood boards are a great way of doing this and are usually images, textures and words placed (gummed usually using spray mount) onto a piece of foam board. You might think this is a ridiculously outdated way of presenting work and that it's a lot easier to do on a touch screen. But what a screen lacks is the tactility of images having been cut out by human hands and stuck on that board. Being able to pass around, hold and point at a board in a client meeting goes a long way to enhancing the emotiveness of what's being explained. You also may be surprised how something produced by hand has more weight on it than something you put together in an electronic presentation. It's the difference between sending someone an e-card for their birthday and making one yourself. We're so used to everything being in electronic form that it's a refreshing change when someone uses or presents something "real."

## Mood boards: E-mail or in person?

There are two very different types of mood boards: those that are e-mailed to the client and are worked up with annotations to be as clear as possible and those that are more free-form in style and are presented to a client. This type of mood board requires the creative involved in putting it together to add their creative spin and take the clients on a journey through the images and text on the board. This requires a little bit of showmanship and can be completely ruined if a well-meaning project manager e-mails the client the mood board ahead of the meeting. This will only confuse them and they'll arrive at the meeting with questions rather than a willingness to have the creative use the mood board to help them share the same creative vision.

## A bunch of stuff shoved together

A common mistake when putting a board together is to throw everything into it. A couple of images that represent a thought or idea are more powerful than ten less powerful ones. Test out your board on a colleague, and if you're having to explain the same points over and over again or having to justify how images connect with one another, reduce the content on the board. Put yourself in the mind-set that you're curating an exhibition that has a common tone and theme. Why some exhibitions work and others don't all comes down to how they've been curated. It's very easy to shove a bunch of stuff together and call it an exhibition, but it's an art form to choose items that have a synergy with one another and tell a story when they are placed together. This is what curating is all about. It's about seeing how meaning and tone can be conveyed. Ask yourself at each image, texture or word choice on your board if it has a right to be there, if it works with the other items. Will it confuse the viewer?

## Tricks of the trade

Large images on boards trigger questions in the viewer's head, which then should receive clarification by placing smaller supporting images around the larger one. A mood board doesn't have to just feature images. Large words work very well, especially if they're juxtaposed together on a board. Remember that the board is there to help put the client into your headspace and be receptive to creative ideas.

## Watch and learn

During any creative presentation, watch your audience's faces. You'll soon know if you're "losing them" or if they're looking confused and bewildered by your ideas. Some people are too polite and will nod their heads in agreement until they get back to the office and tell you with the invisible shield of e-mail that they "just didn't get it." Watch faces and look for confusion. If you see it, act on it with clarification of what you're presenting. You'll eventually see it "click" with them, and the look of confusing turns to understanding. Keep it light-hearted and don't be afraid to ask them to explain back to you in their own words what you've presented.

# The successful creative meeting

**IF YOU'RE PREPARING** a creative meeting don't "bulk out" the meeting by inviting people who shouldn't really be there and whose time would be best spent doing something else. Ask yourself is your meeting (a) a purely conceptual/brainstorming session, or (b) a project update. "A" shouldn't really involve project managers or account directors, as you most probably won't be discussing deliverables, deadlines or budgets. "B" should involve the account director, creative lead, project manager, developer etc. Inviting the wrong type of people to the wrong types of meetings can be disastrous. A blue-skies ideas concept meeting, for example, could turn into:

**Creative:** "So this is a great idea, yeah? How about we have a house that turns into world famous landmarks like the Tower of London or the Taj Mahal and then..."

**Project manager:** "Where would you source the Tower of London image? What would be the cost? How long would we need the rights for?"

**Creative:** "Er..."

**Project manager:** "Is there any way it could turn into the Leaning Tower of Pisa?"

**Developer:** "Is this going to be a 3-D render?"

**Project manager:** Okay, so I need to budget for a 3-D artist? How long would it take to render the Taj Mahal?"

Have the lovely and fluffy creative conversations out of the way before you involve those who need to create timelines and project plans. Meetings aren't made successful by inviting lots of people but instead by inviting the right people.

## Magpie inspiration

Creative meetings shouldn't be about going online and ripping off other people's ideas. For a kickoff creative meeting, try banning any online usage and instead look at the brief and ask each team member to come up with the wackiest, zaniest most off–the-wall idea for the campaign/project. Each of these ideas isn't allowed to associate with an existing campaign or piece of work online or on TV. Nobody is allowed to judge what is said, and each idea is written on a white board. Now look at the brief again and, with the team, discuss in which order the ideas should be categorized as most relevant to the campaign. Now work through them again and come up with a hybrid of all the ideas to make one relevant one.

What you're essentially doing is taking a "blue-skies" idea and bringing it a little bit nearer the ground while retaining the best and most original parts of the original concept. Keep asking the questions "How would the user interact with this?," "How would it work as an app?," "If there were print and television advertising for this, what would be the taglines?" and so on. You'll find that these questions generate solutions that also generate additional questions—all of which fit under the umbrella of the original concept. This is a far more interesting creative discussion that sitting in front of a screen and saying, "Okay, so Amazon is doing this and I noticed that ASOS is displaying their products like this ... So if we do a bit of that and add this functionality that eBay has ..." Now, that's not very original, is it?

## Stand and deliver

If you're doing daily project status updates, think about doing them standing up. None of us like to be on our feet too long and it's a tried-and-true technique for keeping a meeting short.

## Keep it short and prepare

For project status meetings, plan what pertinent points or open issues you want to bring up. If your open issues are liable to take the project status meeting in a different direction—which doesn't involve anyone else there—then agree to continue these discussions during a one-on-one with the relevant person outside of the current meeting. Nobody wants to listen to a person's issues being raked over with a senior member of staff if the issues don't affect them. This is what a one-on-one with your team leader is for, and this type of issue should be reserved for that time.

## The politeness factor

After having presented three creative ideas to a client, there always is a sense of anticlimax afterwards. What we'd love them to do is to burst into applause, screaming, "My God, you're a creative GENIUS" or "These ideas are so good I want to use them ALL." It's an awkward situation for them and you, as they need time to digest what they've heard and seen. They've literally been put on the spot, so don't be disheartened if they want to go off and "get back to you" with their thinking. This is a good thing. Forcing the issue during the meeting will possibly force a few oohs and ahhs out of them but it won't be a considered response. They may even feel the need to be overly critical because of pressure to say something. Give them a bit of time to think.

## Involve the client

After you've locked down a creative concept for a piece of work, don't be afraid of touching base with the client by involving them in creative discussions as the project progresses. Introduce them to the team, involve them in "What do you think?" conversations. This will iron out any potential problems later on and can keep a project on track and on budget.

## Did they just say that?

When presenting to a client, keep the creative team "on the same page" or, as another worn expression puts it, "singing from the same hymn sheet." I've been in pitch meetings where creatives unused to client/agency meeting etiquette have become loose cannons by throwing in new ideas that take a project in a completely new and financially unrealistic creative direction. It's then left to the senior designer or creative lead to manage the (massively raised) client expectations.

# Promote yourself!

**CHANCES ARE**, you show signs of being a digital obsessive. Usual signs are an accelerated heart rate when somebody hits the "Like" button on a piece of your work and a fascination with apps, tech and wanting to be part of the buzz either remotely on creative forums or in person at industry meetups. This is good healthy stuff, as it's good to share your work and have feedback from your peers—even better if the feedback comes from those who don't spend their lives creating or commissioning creative work. You can't beat real world "person on the street" feedback.

Even if you're working away in an agency, it's still good to leave a size 9 digital footprint of yourself and your personal work across the web and—now this may be a shocker—also turning off the computer and indulging in a bit of digerati socializing. Some of the most popular ways to promote your own work include the following.

## Twitter

Tweeting, retweeting and following people who interest you is what Twitter is all about. It has the power to connect you with people and companies you admire that are similar to you or ones you'd like to groom for a while before asking them for a job … Now that's not a bad thing. Following an agency or studio you admire and strategically tweeting your work can raise your profile to them. Don't overdo it, though, as people will become tired if you continuously tweet work, work and more work. Balance it with tweets about where you've been, shows you've seen, the football match, opera and ballet. Real life stuff helps round you out as an interesting person and one who isn't sitting in their bedroom all evening tweeting about their latest pixel-pushing efforts.

Twitter is full of observational commentary, usually delivered in wry one-liners or with a tongue permanently stuck in the tweeter's cheek. Mostly these are entertaining, short and pithy commentaries on life, work and what's good on the telly. Sometimes tweets become similar to "capsule criticism," which is a type of criticism used by theatre and film reviewers to deliver bouquets or brickbats to a show, film or performer by using the shortest possible amount of words to deliver the deftest of blows. A classic example was for the Broadway play "I Am a Camera" by John Van Druten in 1951. In his review of the play, critic Walter Kerr declared his opinion with acerbic wit: "Me no Leica." A sharp and funny line, but one wonders how apt it was for a play that went on to win a much-vaunted Tony award. Perhaps it was just used because it was funny. You'll find clever wordplay like this all over Twitter, with some of it being good and some of it a clever, succinct way of hurling abuse. It's easy to hide behind a device or computer and say bad things about good people trying to do good work in 140 characters or less. Be wise about indulging in some post-booze Friday lunch Twitter clever put-downs. Tweets never die ... They just hang around waiting to explode when you least want them to. You never know who your next boss or client will be or how much they'll Twitter stalk you when considering you for a job, so easy on any zealous put-downs.

## Facebook

Facebook is the equivalent of being a teenager and sticking pictures of your best friends, favorite bands, places you've visited, movies you like and people you fancy up on your bedroom wall and saying to the world, "This is me." Addictive, sometimes facile and generally full of pictures of people with their cats, Facebook nonetheless has enormous digital clout—perfect for attention seekers.

Most creatives groan about creating

**Google loves Facebook in search results so make it love your page even more by adding lots of text and info about what you do and your type of work.**

Facebook fan pages for clients because they're usually bolted on right at the end of a campaign when the client decides "we need a bit of Facebook." It's one of those things clients think they need even if it's not relevant to the campaign because everyone talks about Facebook so it's an easy win to say to their bosses, "Yeah, we're on Facebook," because everyone—tech savvy or not—understands what that is.

Creating a fan page for yourself, though, can reap dividends. Posting your own work on this with a smattering of "what you're up to"-style posts, meetup invites or links to work you like can help raise your profile. They're ridiculously easy to set up as well. Log on to Facebook and at the bottom of the page you'll find a link to "Advertising." Click "Pages" and "Create a Page" and start putting together your page.

Google loves Facebook in search results so make it love your page even more by adding lots of text and info about what you do and your type of work. You can add videos, images and maybe even a mug shot of yourself.

Then comes the hard work, as people won't know about your page unless you shout about it. You probably won't get all 300 million active users to "Like" your page, but you can use it to network by asking your friends to share the link with their friends on Facebook. If a large chunk of your friends work in a related field then it can

be useful to gain some of their contacts for feedback, networking and exposure.

## Instagram

Instagram is an app that allows you to take photos and enhance them with a fake depth of field blur; then you can choose a filter to give the photo a more stylized look. There was once a quote on Twitter about Instagram, saying it was to professional photographers what boob jobs are to large-breasted ladies. Sure, the effects can become stale and overused, but some of the results can be phenomenal. Instagram is less about photos of you and your friends taken at arm's length with a camera phone and more about character, architecture, quirky detail, events and spaces.

You might think, I'm not a photographer so why would this appeal to me? But it's a way of sharing a little bit of your creative universe with people without it directly relating to your work. An eye for an image that has a good bit of juxtaposition in it or a well-composed shot or perhaps a humorous portrait showcase that you're a creative thinker with a good sense of composition and an eye for color and tone. Perfect for what we do for a living.

From the app, you can add followers who can then follow you back. You can find these via Facebook or Twitter or by searching names and user names on Instagram itself. There's a "popular" feed of images that you can trawl through and "Like" or follow that user, which could result in a follow back.

## Blogs and websites

WordPress (http://wordpress.com/) makes it easy to make a nice folio website with loads of free customizable templates available. If you know your CSS from your PHP, you can have a go at custom styles and functions.

Blogs featuring your own work are great, but you need to add something else in order for people to follow you on a regular basis. You could tell the world about your inspiration as well by curating a blog of inspiration, new tech or what's happening on the creative scene, and you're onto a winner. It shows a passion for what's happening in the industry and who is doing what and where. It also makes for interesting reading and will soon rack up subscribers, which of course you can showcase work to in between showing them your sources of interest.

## Events and meetups

Virtual offices and working remotely are great, but we work in a very social industry in which you'll often find organized meetups or socials taking place in your area. If there isn't one, you could, of course, start one. Franz Jeitz explains how he and a few friends set up LDNMeets:

> *It all started in September 2011, when James White (Signalnoise) visited the UK and decided to host his own meetup to connect with all the people he only knew via social media. It was at that meetup up that Ollie, Greg and I met. Having had a brilliant time, we decided to try and do it again, this time without James, though. It took us about three months to take it a bit more seriously, coming up with a name, buying the domain and setting up a mailing list.*

*We've had about six meetups so far and managed to get a great inner circle already, with the likes of Radim Malinic (Brand Nu), Gordon Reid (Middle Boop) and Tom Muller (helloMuller).*

The aim is to have at least one meetup per month, though it's sometimes difficult to settle on a date. It's all very much DIY, but then again, it was never meant to be something super slick. It's all about having a drink and laugh with like-minded people.

There are, of course, the big digital and interactive conferences or "festivals," as they're now being called. The most well known is South by Southwest (http://sxsw.com), which takes place in Austin, Texas, usually around March or April each year. There's also the festival for creative artists, designers and coders, "Reasons to be Creative" (www.reasonstobecreative.com), which is held in New York, London and Brighton. .*net* magazine (www.netmagazine.com) has a very useful monthly calendar of digital and interactive events, which will have you tripping the light fantastic from networking to meetup to interactive festival.

## Left-field creative thinking

You could also use a little bit of left-field thinking to promote yourself and your work. Teacake Design's (http://teacakedesign.com) Graham Sykes and Robert Walmsley were asked to donate an industry event with a prize for a raffle taking place during the evening. Instead of offering a print of their work, a type block or something along those lines, Graham and Robert offered themselves as the prize. The company that "won them" then put them to work on a top notch account, which made Teacake a name with their winners and demonstrated what they could do for a client—showcasing brilliantly some left-field creative thinking.

# Avoiding typecasting with self-initiated work

**PART OF OUR WORK** is about expressing ourselves. The other part is delivering work that fits the client brief. Sometimes this doesn't go hand in hand and can cause frustration on the part of the creative. Quite frankly, trying to express your love of early twentieth-century Maltese art in a campaign for washing powder isn't going to go down well. Shoehorning ideas or graphic treatments simply because you fancy doing something in that style isn't going to be the best solution for the product, service or client. The end creative has to work for the campaign.

Most creatives have bundles of ideas that we're desperate to give life to in some medium or other, but we occasionally hit a brick wall when it comes to using these in our paid work.

Self-initiated work is the answer to rising above the feeling of being creatively stunted in your job. This doesn't mean moonlighting for another agency (well of course you could do that but you risk being found out and burning your bridges at your current agency) but rather spending your own time working on ideas or projects or taking time out to understand a new skill that your day-to-day job doesn't afford you the time to do. It's a great way to keep you creatively challenged and to try out new techniques and work approaches, which can then be fed into your agency work. It's also a great litmus test of any creative. Like we've touched on before, being a creative is an enduring passion and one not constrained by the nine-to-five grind. It's this around-the-clock passion, pig-headedness or sheer need to express an idea that, as Johnny Issacs puts it, "shows that you genuinely love what you do rather than just doing it for a monthly paycheck."

You could take an existing campaign and rework it (politically it's best to take one from another agency so as to not to bruise

> **I believe self-initiated work is less about keeping your skills fresh and more about keeping yourself fulfilled creatively. For too many years I made the mistake of relying on clients to determine the fate of my creative output.**
>
> — Brian Hurewitz

the ego of anyone you work with). Approach the brief from your direction and see where that takes you. You could take all those blue-sky ideas of yours that haven't seen daylight and give them another look. Dust them off, develop them and make them viable and workable. You might think, Well, what's the point?, but all this work will stand you in good stead moving forward through your career. It shows passion, bolsters out the online portfolio and shows a breadth of knowledge. All of these are great showcases of what you can do, and by doing them, you've added more feathers to your creative cap. Rachel Shillcock explains:

> *Working on self-initiated work means you can explore and have SO much fun! Personal projects are a great way of unleashing your imagination and pushing your creativity to its limits. A fun thing to do, as well, is to try and figure out what product or service is missing in your life that you would use—and then try and create a fun project to do with that. You never know; it might even be useful for more than just yourself and help raise your profile!*

If you struggle with creative typecasting, then doing your own personal work will help push you out of this. If you find yourself being labeled as the "go-to guy" for graphics but you want to break into animation, then doing your own work can help bridge that gap. The next time an animation brief comes into the studio, you can try your hand at it and use your own self-initiated work as testament to your being able to do the work.

# Contributors

**LEON BAHRANI** is a senior designer with eight years experience at award-winning brand agency The Partners in London. While at The Partners, Leon has helped create and deliver effective brand communications for a diverse range of clients across multiple sectors, including the BBC, the Royal Mail, The National Gallery, Novo Nordisk and HSBC.

He has been frequently awarded in leading design competitions within the creative industry, both domestic and international. After studying graphic design at the BA (Hons) level, he gained a master's degree from the London College of Communication.

**www.the-partners.com**

**BEN POWELL** is an up-and-coming UI and graphic designer based in Sheffield. He has worked on mobile app designs for the likes of AXA, Unilever and Royal Caribbean, as well as hotel chain De Vere Village. His recent "I am who I am because of everyone" project was exhibited in South Yorkshire and also featured in *Computer Arts* magazine. By day, he works at the software developer 3Squared, and by night, he follows his passion for personal projects and freelance work.

**www.gogetcreative.co.uk**

An art director by trade, **BRIAN HUREWITZ** has spent over a decade crafting integrated campaigns and digital experiences for clients including Kodak, IKEA, Tylenol and Johnson & Johnson. After gaining experience at agencies such as Deutsch, he moved on to become creative director at Swedish digital agency Great Works, during which time he helped launch Yves Saint Laurent's Belle d'Opium fragrance and rebrand and relaunch Kahlúa. Brian's work has been recognized by *Communication Arts*, *Adweek*, PSFK, the Art Directors Club and FWA.

Most recently, he opened Brook&Lyn Studio with his wife Mimi Jung. They combined their experience in design, fashion and technology with their innate sense of style to form a modern, multidisciplinary creative studio. In April, they relocated from NY to LA with plans to open a retail experience in the fall of 2012.

**http://brianhurewitz.com**

**CAROLINE ANNIS** has worked in the digital media industry for twenty years in a variety of creative roles such as designer, editor, project manager and strategist. She has a breadth of industry experience with broadcasters such as Sky and the BBC, commercial and public sector organizations, advertisers, retailers and niche communities. She works with clients to design and deliver services and strategies that bring about multichannel change.

**www.annis.co**

Planning Unit was established Feb 2011, founded by **NICK HARD** and **JEFF KNOWLES.** In the short time since setting up, they have had the opportunity to work for a great range of clients, including the BBC, Knoll, Design Museum, D&AD, Bonfire Snowboarding, Salomon, *Twin* magazine, pq Eyewear (Ron Arad), Paris Saint-Germain F.C. and Xindao amongst others.

**http://planningunit.co.uk/**

**JOSEPH R. LUCK** is currently a full-time student studying sound design at Ravensbourne College of Design and Communication. Joe believes that having a degree isn't enough to guarantee work in a creative industry; he thinks that experience is equally, if not more desirable. He also specializes in web design and development. He's a guitar and game hobbyist. In conjunction with university study, he provides a range of audio and web services through Joseph Luck Design. His clients include the RSA, Future Publishing, Made by Many, Knight Studios, Awake-London and Enigmati Inc. Outside of audio, Joe has a portfolio primarily of personal and small business websites.

**www.josephluck.co.uk**

**MIRANDA BOLTER** joined The Partners as a designer in 2007 and has since worked on some award-winning projects including Fine Cell Work and Mr. Singh's Bangras.
Before joining The Partners, Miranda spent ten years in

marketing within the food and hospitality industry. Since joining The Partners, she has worked with a wide range of clients including Deloitte, Sophos, the NHS and Vodafone. Miranda's work has been widely recognized by New York Festivals, Design Week Awards, Clio Awards and Cannes Lions. **www.the-partners.com**

**BEN CURZON** hung around Camden being in some bands and working at grotty live venues before falling into designing record covers for arcane electronic labels and populous-pleasing pop-popsicles. He then stumbled over a typography epiphany and gingerly toward being something of a real graphic designer for around ten years. He mourned the death of Macromedia Freehand and traversed a vast and hazy fissure to become a UI and User Experience designer along a path toward infinitely evolving digital innovation nirvana.

**NATALIE HUNTER** was co-founder of legendary creative agency Airside, which she co-ran 1998 to 2012. She currently holds a joint role at the Royal Society of Arts as Director of Design and also as Director at Tokyo Digital.

**PETER KNAPP** is Landor's Global Creative Officer, based in the London studio. He has been at Landor for more than nineteen years. Starting in the London office, he subsequently moved to the Hong Kong office for a few

years where he had overall responsibility for steering and directing all branding programs in Southeast Asia. As well as being very actively involved in some of Landor's landmark clients, he is also working with the global management team to establish a new creative era for the company.

He specializes in integrated branding programs where graphic, 3-D, digital and engagement design platforms are fused together to form total branded experiences for consumers and has accumulated a very broad range of branding experience across markets, geographies and disciplines.

Peter is widely known for his unparalleled expertise in airline branding, from flag carriers to low-cost brands where the entire customer journey is studied to yield unique customer interfaces and moments. He also has a broad range of experience in other industries, including automotive, petroleum, spirits, financial services, telecommunications, retail, and leisure. Some of his clients include Marks & Spencer, BP, De Beers, Diageo, Ernst & Young, Hang Seng Bank, Land Rover, Maybourne Hotel Group, Morrisons, Preem, bmi, Gulf Air, S7 and British Airways.

He is a regular contributor to the national and trade press on brand topics and has contributed to various books and broadcasts on branding and is often asked to judge at international awards such as Cannes, D&AD and Design Week. An alternative description would be: a proud Londoner, a suffering West Ham Utd supporter and a real design geek.

**LOU CORDWELL** started her career working for a number of large multinational ad agencies before founding interactive design company magneticNorth in the summer of 2000. Since then she has led the business from its original team of four to a now internationally renowned business and brand with a multiaward-winning portfolio of work and a blue chip client list that includes the BBC, ARUP, Reuters and Marketing Manchester. In February 2011, Lou co-founded a products company, Beep Industries, whose portfolio includes the MoviePeg (www.movie-peg.com) and POPA (www.thisispopa.com) brands. In October 2011, Lou returned in a full-time capacity to mN in the role of CEO. Lou also has a number of prestigious business awards to her name, including 'Manchester Young Director of the Year' from the IoD, and in 2010, she was named both 'Digital Entrepreneur' and 'Female Entrepreneur of the Year' by *Entrepreneur* magazine.

**www.mnatwork.com**

**ADAM TODD** has more than fourteen years' experience working in interactive design. He joined mN in 2005 and now heads up the interactive design team where he focuses on creating digital experiences that charm and engage audiences. In the last twelve months, Adam and his team have collaborated with the BBC on projects including the Desert Island Discs site, which has had over five million downloads since it launched in April and 'Maestro', an interactive installation using Microsoft Kinect, which gave children the opportunity to conduct the BBC Philharmonic orchestra. They are currently working with BBC Sport on a large-scale project for mobile.

**www.mnatwork.com**

After completing his degree, **PAUL DAVIS** began freelancing as an illustrator and animator in London in 2005 for editorial, commercial and independent clients. Interested in all aspects of design, Paul developed a range of design skills from typography to web design and launched himself on the London design scene. He was hired by an agency based out of an old tobacco factory in Farringdon and then spent the next two years working with various top agencies as a multiskilled freelance designer.

In 2007, Paul started a freelance role at Overthrow Digital with his friend and soon-to-be business partner Jim Towning. Paul is now a partner at Overthrow Digital, where he continues to bring his unique design skills and creative flair to all manner of web and digital projects.

**contact | paul@overthrowproductions.com**

**STEVE ALEXANDER** is a client-facing, creative web developer with more than fifteen years experience in the industry and the gray hairs to prove it. His forte is developing stimulating, innovative web solutions and experimenting with the latest technologies.

He has worked in a variety of environments, from the early days with an Internet start-up, working flat out as a freelancer and running his own web design business, through the glory days with well-known Internet portal Lycos, to the present day with digital agency GLG London (http://glg-london.com). He's constantly amazed that, more than ten years from its release, he's still having to test things in Internet Explorer 6.

When not staring at screens in an office, he's kept busy in leafy Hertfordshire with his wife and three-year-old son/alarm clock.

**http://5cubed.com**

**NATALIE JAHANGIRY** graduated from Northumbria University in Multimedia Design in 2008 and became a London-based designer shortly after this. Her time in the industry so far has seen her delivering successful design communication solutions for well-known organizations such as Virgin Media, the BBC, Disney, NSPCC, Burger King, UNICEF, Bacardi, Cadbury and Sky. Natalie currently works for a large global agency based in West London on a range of media from print and DM to social, mobile and web.

**www.nataliejahangiry.com**

**FRANZ JEITZ** is a 26-year-old freelance graphic designer. Originally from Luxembourg, he's been based in London for the last seven years. He specializes in graphics for the music industry and is the in-house designer for the indie label Communion Records. Franz also runs the design blog at www.fudgegraphics.com, which provides quality freebies and features the latest talents in the design scene.

A member of the National Union of Journalists and the Chartered Institute of Public Relations, **JANET AWE** has worked in the communications industry for nearly twenty years. During that time, she's immersed herself in the business of creativity, using the tools in her arsenal to bring out the best in her clients and demonstrate the benefits their products and services can deliver. Janet prefers to work with a cross section of clients and is delighted that the industries she's worked successfully in include film and media, fashion and music, travel and education. From creating fully integrated PR and marketing strategies, social media campaigns and events, to working as a freelance journalist, particularly covering the arts, Janet enjoys the creative process in any form.

**www.awesomecomms.com**

**JOHNNY ISAACS** is a director at Explosive Brands Limited, which he started in March 2012 after working for a mid-sized creative agency specializing in mobile web and app design. He works creating branding and moving image primarily, though he is always looking for an excuse to bust out the pencils and start drawing some typefaces.

**www.explosivebrands.com**

Since joining The Partners in 2010, **ROSS FORDHAM** has worked on a number of flagship projects for Deloitte, including the design and installation of an anamorphic branded environment at the 2011 World Economic Forum in Davos. He is currently leading the design team on the brand evolution of Kenyan telecom giant Safaricom. Ross previously worked at Salter Baxter and Dave, where he spent 3.5 years working on multichannel branding programs for clients such as Channel 5, Hunter, Sub Zero & Wolf and Vertu. Ross has freelance experience working in the beauty and fashion industry and spent six months building a wooden house in Sussex.

Ross is a regular media commentator and judges on a variety of awards including D&AD.

**www.the-partners.com**

**RACHEL SHILLCOCK** is a designer and front-end developer from Manchester, UK. She is a published logo designer and writer, appearing in books and magazines such as *Logo Design Volume 3* and *.net* magazine. Rachel has worked as a web designer and front-end developer for agencies in Manchester, including an SEO agency and full-service agency, as well as freelancing for local and online businesses and personalities. In her spare time, Rachel is a photography enthusiast, and she enjoys taking long walks around the countryside with her camera and tripod in hand.

**www.rachil.li.**

**SAMANTHA PELIZA** has extensive experience in producing and project managing digital content for ITV, Virgin Media, Burberry and *The Guardian*. Specializing in branded campaigns, she has delivered cross-platform projects uniting print, online and TV for the likes of Nike, Estée Lauder and Sony BMG. Her passion for organizing has seen her set up creative solution departments and processes, "ensuring workflow harmony." Sam loves the industry for the different personalities she gets to work with and the evolving nature of digital arts. She motivates her creative teams by feeding them cookies and chili sauce (but not at the same time).

**contact | sampeliza@yahoo.co.uk**

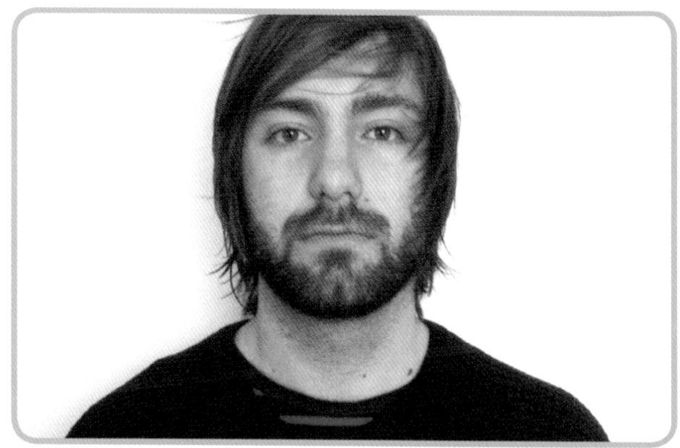

**ALEX HARDING** comes from a small village outside of London called Much Hadham and went to Buckinghamshire Uni to study multimedia design, but a few months after his studies, he joined Crab Creative, a digital agency based in Shoreditch, London, before moving to Made by Many, who specialize in creating products and services for clients such as ITV and Skype.

Made by Many's interaction designer **TOM HARDING** transforms business requirements into practical and desirable experiences using his sketching and prototype skills.

He understands user needs and the technology, which are both essential during the creation process. Beardy man. Comic fan. Tech whore. Lover of maps. Tom is not a rock-star or a guru.

**http://madebymany.com/**

Growing up in sunny Bognor Regis and looking out across the sea kind of drills into you the question: "What's over the horizon?" And going for a scout or a wade, swim or adventure into the unknown is exciting and **DANNY WHITFIELD** recommends it for an attitude when taking on what at first may seem challenging projects.

Currently head of digital for the soaps at ITV, Danny has been working in television and the visual arts for ten years. He comes from a more theatrical and performance-based background and is never afraid to throw this experience into winning new projects and being inventive around new media.

Danny's advice: "Go learn how to record things, edit them a bit and present them to an audience and you shall inherit the earth."

**TOM BAKER** is a 2-D character animator and illustrator. In addition to working in-house on various larger projects (e.g., contracts on TV shows, etc.) he operates as a one-man agency providing short animation solutions for TV ads, infomercials, websites, computer games, TV shows, etc.

**http://bakeranimator.com**

**MILLS** co-founded ustwo™ back in 2004 with business partner sinx. Their aim was to build a studio where like-minded creatives could share unique ideas and bring them to life. As ustwo's CHIEF WONKA™, mills literally lives and breathes mobile as the self-proclaimed King of Succailure.™ He has launched creative apps that have sold globally in their hundreds. If you're interested in the truth, then follow @millsustwo. If not, follow him anyway.

**www.ustwo.co.uk**

**www.youtube.com/watch?v=z7Z3qXDPDDY**

# About the Author

**PAUL WYATT** is a creative director, writer and film maker based in London, England. He's produced short films, websites, apps and brand identity creative for clients such as the Royal Society of Arts, the BBC, the Royal Academy of Music, Cadbury, Virgin Media, Daft Punk, Playstation, Adobe and the D&AD.

Paul contributes a monthly column to *.net* magazine and presented the *.net* magazine vodcast "Web design TV" which ran for fifty episodes between 2008 and 2010. He regularly writes for the design blog *Creative Bloq* and writes reviews, opinion pieces and features for websites, magazines and newspapers.

Paul is a regular contributor of articles to the world's best-selling creative magazine *Computer Arts* as well as having produced and filmed their *Studio Life* series, which took a peak behind the scenes at some of the world's best design and branding agencies. An industry veteran, Paul has been on the judging panel of ITV's design challenge series *Whose London?* as well as a judge for international design tournament Cut&Paste and the *.net* magazine awards.

Paul combines his creative and journalistic skills with producing short films. An accomplished documentary maker, Paul produced *The Story of Picle* for Made by Many and most recently has been filming a series of short films for the Royal Society of Arts Great Recovery project, which examines how important it is for products to be designed so they have a second life.

**www.paulwyatt.co.uk**

# Permissions

*Discovery Channel/Singapore Airlines,* project images © 2012 Why Not Associates Ltd. http://whynotassociates.com

*Whale Trail,* project images © 2012 ustwo™ studio Ltd. http://www.ustwo.co.uk

*Desert Island Discs,* project images printed with permission from BBC Radio 4 © 2013, created by magneticNorth http://mnatwork.com

Valor, project images © 2012 Made by Many Ltd. http://madebymany.com

*Just Rosie,* project images © 2011 ITV www.itvstudios.com

Microsoft Surface Experience, project images © 2012 magneticNorth http://mnatwork.com

*The War Horse Journey,* project images © 2012 Shoothill http://www.shoothill.com

All other images appear courtesy of the contributors.

# Index

# More Great Titles from HOW Books

## The Designer's Web Handbook

By Patrick McNeil

Web guru Patrick McNeil teaches you the fundamentals of great web design. He explains how to make a website not only look good, but work as well. Too many designers are unaware of the differences they'll face when designing for the web. Things like efficient navigation and building for easy updates or changes may be neglected in the planning process. This book will help you avoid making those costly mistakes so that your designs work the way you want them to.

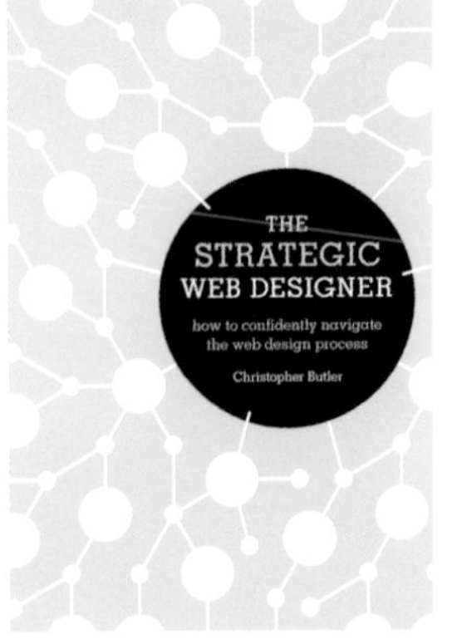


## The Strategic Web Designer

By Christopher Butler

This indispensible guide teaches you how to think about the web, and prepares you to lead web projects from the critical inception phase through to the ongoing nurturing process every website needs. That's what web strategy is all about: having a comprehensively informed point of view on the web that enables you to guide a web project intentionally, rather than reactively. More than a book about building websites, *The Strategic Web Designer* is your guide to thinking about the web in a strategic and comprehensive manner. Be more than just a web designer—take charge of your web projects and make yourself invaluable to your clients.

***Find these books and many others at MyDesignShop.com or your local bookstore.***

## Special Offer From HOW Books!

You can get **15% off** your entire order at **MyDesignShop.com!** All you have to do is go to **www.howdesign.com/howbooks-offer** and sign up for our free e-newsletter on graphic design. You'll also get a **free digital download** of HOW magazine.

FOR MORE NEWS, tips and articles, follow us at Twitter.com/HOWbrand

FOR BEHIND-THE-SCENES INFORMATION and special offers, become a fan at Facebook.com/HOWmagazine

FOR VISUAL INSPIRATION, follow us at Pinterest.com/HOWbrand